The Service Industries in a Developing Economy

PRAEGER SPECIAL STUDIES IN
INTERNATIONAL ECONOMICS AND DEVELOPMENT

The Service Industries in a Developing Economy

ISRAEL AS A CASE STUDY

Gur Ofer

Published in cooperation with
the Bank of Israel

by

FREDERICK A. PRAEGER, Publishers
New York · Washington · London

The purpose of the Praeger Special Studies is to make specialized research monographs in U.S. and international economics and politics available to the academic, business, and government communities. For further information, write to the Special Projects Division, Frederick A. Praeger, Publishers, 111 Fourth Avenue, New York, N.Y. 10003.

FREDERICK A. PRAEGER, PUBLISHERS
111 Fourth Avenue, New York, N.Y. 10003, U.S.A.
77-79 Charlotte Street, London W.1, England

Published in the United States of America in 1967
by Frederick A. Praeger, Inc., Publishers

© 1967 by the Bank of Israel

Library of Congress Catalog Card Number: 66-27961

Printed in Israel at the Jerusalem Post Press, Jerusalem

This book is one of a series of studies carried out under the guidance of the Advisory Council for the Israel Economic and Sociological Research Project, set up in close cooperation with the List Institute, Basle.

The author and publishers express their appreciation to Professor Edgar Salin of the University of Basle, who initiated the project, to the List Institute and its director, Professor H. W. Zimmermann, and to the Israel Advisory Council, for the guidance, encouragement and financial aid which made this study possible.

Acknowledgements

THIS STUDY, an early version of which was submitted to the Hebrew University, Jerusalem as an M.A. thesis, was written during 1963 and 1964.

I am happy to express my deep gratitude to Dr Nadav Halevi for his constant guidance throughout its preparation. I am also most grateful to Professor Simon Kuznets who kindly read an early draft of this study and from whose many constructive comments I benefited greatly. Dr R. Klinov-Malul, Professor M. Michaely, Dr E. Kleiman and Professor A. Morag of the Hebrew University, and Dr A. L. Gaathon of the Bank of Israel also made helpful comments on the first draft.

I am especially indebted to Susanne Freund, who contributed much to the study in translating it from the Hebrew, editing it, and guiding it through the stages of publication. I also thank Rachel Shapiro who saw the study through the press.

The research was made possible by a grant from the Advisory Council for the Israel Economic and Sociological Research Project (in cooperation with the List Institute, Basle), to which I extend my thanks.

Finally, I would like to record my thanks to the Bank of Israel which undertook the publication of this study.

GUR OFER

Harvard University
September 1966

Contents

List of Tables

Abbreviations and Symbols

CBS   Central Bureau of Statistics
FP   Falk Project for Economic Research in Israel
GNP   Gross national product
ISIC   International Standard Industrial Classification
LFS   Labour Force Survey
LP   Palestine pounds
NAD   National Accounts Division of CBS
NBER   National Bureau of Economic Research
NDP   Net domestic product
PTT   Post, Telephone, Telegraph
SAI   Statistical Abstract of Israel
SBI   Statistical Bulletin of Israel
–   zero
0   less than half last digit shown
xx   not relevant
..   not available

Chapter 1: Introduction

1. THE STRUCTURE OF THE STUDY

A country's economic structure—the industrial distribution of national product and of labour force and other inputs—and its level of development are closely bound up, and influence one another as they change. Economic structure is also linked with social patterns, such as the degree of urbanization, and the demographic and class structures. A study of Israel's industrial structure must concern itself with these general aspects. In addition, however, it must respond to the normative aspect of whether or not this structure is 'healthy' in relation to the Zionist ideology, one of whose main principles was the so-called 'inversion of the occupational pyramid'—that is, the conversion of the strongly services-oriented industrial and occupational structure of Diaspora Jews to a 'normal' one based on what has been called a productive economy. This aim has been justified both in terms of 'optimum' or 'healthy' economic structure, and in terms of social and national values.

To those interested in the success of the Zionist ideology, an important criterion is the share of services, often stated to be excessive in Israel: there are frequent calls to return to productive activities, and to 'heal' the economy. Both the assertion and the suggested solution take it for granted that activity in services is unproductive and akin to thriftlessness.

The purpose of the present work is to describe and analyse, primarily according to economic criteria, the share of services in the Israel economy at present and during the last thirty years. In particular, we attempt to explain why the share is higher in Israel than in some other countries.

The connexion between economic structure and the level of development has been the one most extensively explored in both historical and international cross-section studies. In this introductory chapter we remark only that a close and consistent relationship has been found between various structural features and the growth rates and level of per capita income in various countries, and that there is broad agreement among scholars on the salient features of the relationship.

In general, this work—which is concerned primarily with Israel—will accept the conclusions of the various international comparisons; in some instances, however, we employ tests and suggest explanations of the processes examined which supplement those given elsewhere.

The descriptive and analytical parts of the book are divided into

1

two: we first (Chapters 2 and 3) survey and attempt to explain the situation at a point in time—in our case, around the year 1961—and we then deal with the developments throughout the period 1931 to 1961 (Chapters 4 and 5). The description of changes over time necessarily covers a wider canvas; on the other hand, in the analysis more space will be devoted to the present structure of the economy.

Chapters 2 and 4 deal with the level of the various indicators of industrial structure in general, and of services in particular, and compare Israel at different periods (Chapter 4) and with other countries (Chapter 2); the principal standard of comparison is the level of development or one of its statistical expressions—per capita national income. In Chapters 3 and 5 we attempt to explain the structural differences found in terms of economic, social, and other factors peculiar to Israel, and which mostly stem from the specific circumstances of the country. Comparison is also made with similar situations which other countries have from time to time experienced.

Our use of the comparative approach in general, and the per capita income criterion in particular, is justified because we feel that there is common ground for the comparison with other countries despite the unusual events that have occurred in Palestine-Israel during the last thirty years—the change of regime, demographic changes, and so on. Some, at least, of the principal economic processes show a fair degree of regularity and continuity over the period; there cannot, of course, be absolute comparability in all respects.

The approach of this work is mainly global: aggregate indicators are examined without entering into micro-economic discussions. There is no doubt that greater penetration in depth can contribute a great deal to the elucidation of much that is at present obscure, and one of the purposes of this work is to provide a background and to suggest the chief problems that remain to be more thoroughly gone into in the future.

Changes in the industrial structure of an economy consist of historical processes occurring over several decades; this is true even when dynamic social, technological, demographic, or economic developments take place. It is therefore difficult to discuss such changes in terms of short periods or single years. This is especially true of services, whose share in the industrial structure changes more slowly than that of agriculture or manufacturing. These considerations make it necessary to choose as long a period as possible, and thirty years is by no means too long.

The choice of the population-census years 1931 and 1961 as the limits of our period was dictated both by the nature of the problem and by the statistics available. However, any attempt to cover thirty years raises many difficulties and doubts. To extend a study backwards to the pre-State period exacts a very high—conceptual and technical—'price.' There have been marked demographic, political, and geographical changes in the last thirty years; this makes it doubtful if the period was one of normal and continuous development. From the technical point of view, the pre-State data are less reliable than those of the last decade, and, in most cases, differ from them considerably in definition. Nevertheless, it is possible to find an element of continuity in the economic development of the Jewish sector during the whole period, and this justifies extending the period of the study.

This element was the process of settling immigrants in a new country, accompanied by a persistent quest for the resources required for economic existence and the expansion of the absorption potential. At the same time, it is clear that any analysis and comparison must take account of the significant changes in the conditions underlying the functioning of the Jewish economy.

Our starting point is 1931, when a comprehensive population census was carried out which provided much information on the industrial and occupational structure of Jewish (and other) employed persons. There are earlier figures, [1] but we believe that there are advantages in beginning from a solid and reliable benchmark.

Furthermore, for the Jewish sector of Palestine, the period is not too short. The considerable additions of labour and capital inputs and the rapid rate of growth enabled structural changes to appear within a short period. Clearly, if there is a large annual increment of manpower, the industrial structure of the labour force may change more rapidly than if the population is static. In the latter case some industries must contract in order to make manpower available to expanding branches; with a growing population it is sufficient for the increment to be allocated to the expanding branches for their share to rise.

2. HISTORICAL SURVEY

We shall summarize briefly the principal social, demographic political and economic changes which occurred during our period.

The Jewish population rose from about 175,000 in 1931 to about

[1] See A. Nizan, "The Structure of the Labour Force in the Israel Economy," *Economic Quarterly*, 9–10, October 1955 (Hebrew).

2 million in 1961, or about twelve-fold. The number of employed persons rose from about 65,000 to more than 650,000.

National income rose 14–15 times, and per capita income rose about 2.5 times. [2]

Throughout the period, capital imports were considerable, most of them used for investment purposes, especially in the Jewish sector. This was reflected in a permanent deficit on the current balance of payments, which constituted a large share of the Jewish sector's resources.

Other changes are those which break the thirty years into sub-periods, the chief, though not the only, turning point being the establishment of the State.

During the Mandate, Jews were a minority, active in only part of the economy. It is only since 1948 that the Jewish sector has accounted for more than 90 per cent of the economy, and for roughly 90 per cent of the population. The Jewish sector differed and was separate from the Arab sector, and functioned more or less as a closed economy, whose relations with the other sectors resembled international trade. [3] In our analysis we attempt to take account of these intersectoral connexions.

With the establishment of the State, the country was partitioned. This was not in itself very important for the Jewish sector, which was concentrated mainly in districts which became Israel.

With the change of regime, the burden of central government, including the setting up of a defence force, fell on the Jewish sector. There was a radical change in the government's economic and social policy, both because of mass immigration, and because the new authorities had a fundamentally different conception of the role of government in the economy and in the provision of public services. The new climate was reflected in the growth of the Jewish civil service, and in the great increase in the share of public budgets in total resources. The direction and character of economic ties with the rest of the world changed. Relations with the neighbouring countries were broken off,

---

[2] 1936 to 1961, according to a crude calculation.

[3] See R.R. Nathan, O. Gass, and D. Creamer, *Palestine: Problem and Promise,* Public Affairs Press, Washington, 1946. P.J. Loftus, Government Statistician in the 1940's, writes: "It is of fundamental importance to note that for all important economic purposes, Palestine contains two distinct economies ... [so] that it is necessary to carry into the economic field the distinction between the two races ...," in *National Income of Palestine 1944,* Government Printer, 1946, p. 24.

and an extreme protectionist policy accompanied by various export-boosting devices was initiated.

Although the second world war in a sense constituted a digression, it had a decisive effect on the economy. On the one hand, citrus-growing was seriously affected, and on the other, the war provided opportunities for industrial production. Moreover, the war forced the mandatory government—for military and economic reasons—to increased intervention in the economic system, and led to the closing of the frontiers, with all that this implies. In these two respects, at least, the second world war was a transition period from the 1930's to the establishment of the State.

3. DEFINITIONS

In this work, services comprise (unless otherwise stated) transportation, production and distribution of water, electricity and sanitation services; trade; banking and finance; public (general government, education, health, welfare, religion, etc.) and business (architecture, accountancy and allied occupations) services; and personal services which include domestic service, catering, laundries, and other personal services.[4]

The structural indicators which we shall use to determine the share of services are: (1) the share of national income originating in services (at current prices); (2) the share of persons employed in services; and (3) relative product per employed person. [5] The last is a very crude measure of the relative efficiency of each branch; it refers both to the productivity of labour itself, and to the additional product per worker which stems from changes in input of capital per worker. In each case the data will be presented (where possible, for each service industry separately) at a point in time (1961) and also in a time series for the last thirty years. The industrial allocation of other factors of production falls beyond the scope of this study.

We do not attempt to obtain more than usually refined figures. For example, we make no attempt to standardize the employment figures to take account of differences in hours worked, nor do we attempt to solve conceptual problems such as those connected with the product-worker ratio.

[4] Our classification is usually based on that currently used by the CBS: *Classification of Economic Branches,* which is based on ISIC, adapted to local requirements. For details, see Appendix A.

[5] For brevity we shall refer to (1) product share, (2) employment share, and (3) product per worker or the product-worker ratio.

The principal difficulty in determining the income originating in services is to define income originating in the services of general government and nonprofit institutions. Conventionally, the latter is taken as compensation of employees and some interest payments; interest on the public debt is not usually included in the national income. This definition is defective compared with that used for other branches in that it takes no account of the profit element, nor is any value imputed to capital services; this renders meaningless the relation between actual output, (which should be measured by the value of services supplied), and the compensation of employees supplying the services. In so far as there is a 'true' profit, the conventional method of measurement will result in an underestimate of income originating, while where there is a loss, there will be an overestimate. There may be a bias, and it may vary between the points of observation (different countries or periods); this must be borne in mind.

Product per employed person (the product-worker ratio) is measured by the ratio:

$$\frac{\text{per cent of national product originating in the industry}}{\text{per cent of employed persons in the industry}}.$$

This rough measure raises several conceptual problems.

First, product accruing to share and bond holders and other investors not actively engaged in the industry is included. The income obtained is therefore not precisely that produced by those employed and active in the industry. Owing to lack of data, we cannot use the concept of 'participation income'[6] which excludes returns to capital of inactive owners from income; some progress in this direction is made by excluding from our calculations the income from ownership of dwellings. In any case, the information is also missing from the data of the other countries dealt with, so that for our international comparisons we were forced to revert to the more global and less accurate figures.

Second, the problem of defining income originating in the public sector and nonprofit institutions exists here too, and will bias the product-worker ratio in the same way.

[6] S. Kuznets, "Quantitative Aspects of the Economic Growth of Nations, III. Industrial Distribution of Income and Labor Force by States, United States, 1919–1921 to 1955," *Economic Development and Cultural Change*, Vol. VI, No. 4 Part II, July 1958, p. 3.

4. PROBLEMS OF THE DATA

We here comment only briefly on the chief difficulties:

a. There was neither uniformity nor continuity of data collection throughout our period. The series were compiled from data which had been collected in varying ways (censuses, surveys, estimates), according to different definitions depending on the aspect analysed, and using different economic classifications.

b. There were sometimes no estimates of national product corresponding to the labour force estimates.

c. For services, the classification used for employed persons differs from that used for national product. In order to obtain the product-worker ratios classification adjustments were made wherever possible. [7]

d. Many rough estimates had to be made in order to complete tables or to adapt them to our purpose.

e. The comparison of a long time series with the data for other countries presented a special problem. The comparison is subject to all the usual reservations about inconsistency of definition, method of data-collection, etc. Where possible, we used data which had already been brought together in single studies, and whose compilers had attempted to present them on a common basis. We also made most of our comparisons with groups of countries, on the ground that an average is likely to mask some of the inter-country divergences which arise from differences in methods and definitions and from other errors.

It is therefore desirable to open this study by warning the reader that the data for Israel (especially for the mandatory period and the early years of the State), are often of doubtful reliability.

[7] See Appendix B.

Chapter 2: The Share of Services and Per Capita Income

In this chapter we describe the industrial structure of Israel in 1961, and then apply the per capita income criterion to an international comparison.

1. THE SHARE OF SERVICES IN ISRAEL: 1961

Domestic product

Israel's net domestic product in 1961 is shown in Table 2.1. The industry classification differs from that of the National Accounts Division (NAD) of the CBS because of the following conceptual adjustments:

a. The institutional classification of public services generally used in national accounting here and abroad has been replaced by a functional classification. Product originating in each sub-branch therefore includes that of general government, nonprofit institutions, and enterprises. [1] The classification chosen was one which fitted as closely as possible that of the employment data, which appeared more suitable for most of the purposes of this work. Accordingly, 'productive' activities of general government were also transferred to the appropriate branches.

b. Since the sub-branch data for 1961 are incomplete, the latest available detail (for 1959) was extrapolated where necessary. We can plausibly assume that this procedure does not result in any serious bias when applied over a short period.

In 1961, 51.3 per cent of net domestic product originated in non-dwelling services (ownership of dwellings accounted for another 5.8 per cent). About half of the product originating in services came from public and personal services, [2] while the other half originated in distributive services (transportation, public utilities and trade) and in finance. The bulk of distributive and personal services is supplied by enterprises; most of the income from public services, however, originates in general government agencies (as opposed to profit-making enterprises) or in nonprofit institutions. This cross-classification—by supplier and by type

---

[1] For details of this and other adjustments see Appendix B.
[2] Branch and sub-branch descriptions have been abridged in both text and tables. See Appendix A for the coverage of each description.

8

of service—and its implications are significant from several points of view, including that of the conceptual problems raised in Chapter 1.

Employed persons

The industrial structure of the Jewish civilian employed labour force is shown in Tables 2.2 and 2.3 according to two sources. The main differences between these tables and Table 2.1 (product) are evident from the definitions. The employment data do not on the whole include persons corresponding to the item ownership of dwellings in the product table since this gives rise to a negligible amount of employment. The Census and Surveys (LFS) data are not in full agreement, either in absolute terms or in terms of industrial distribution; the principal divergence is in agriculture, and this accounts for most of the difference in the per cent distribution. A discussion of the discrepancies between the two sources is beyond the scope of this work, but it has elsewhere been indicated that, at least as far as agriculture is concerned, the Surveys are closer to the truth. [3] The other divergences are fairly small, and we consider them as giving the possible range within which the true distribution falls.

The Arab labour force has its own typical branch structure, despite some integration with the Jewish sector, and because many goods and services are supplied by the latter. The principal difference between the two employment patterns is the high concentration of non-Jewish employed persons in agriculture (Table 2.2), and their low share in government and other public services. Nevertheless, since the non-Jewish labour force is only a small part of the total (about 8 per cent), there is not much difference between the figures for Jewish and all employed persons.

In 1961, just over half of Jewish civilian employed persons were employed in services: of these, about 46 per cent were employed in public services (including general government), about 40 per cent in distributive services and finance, and the remaining 14 per cent in personal services. Table 2.3 shows Jewish employment in greater detail. It should be noted that product originating in personal services includes the imputed incomes of service workers in kibbutzim (e.g. in the kitchen and dining-hall, crèches, clothing store), and these workers are also included in the labour force figures. However, their work for the most

[3] A limited attempt to explain the differences may be found in CBS, *Labour Force Part I,* Population and Housing Census 1961 Publication No. 9, 1963, pp. xxxiii ff.

TABLE 2.1   *Industrial[a] Origin of Net Domestic Product:[b] 1961*

	Per cent of	
	Total NDP	NDP originating in services
Total (in IL million)	4,318.1	
A. Total	**100.0**	
Agriculture	10.9	
Industry	24.7	
Construction	7.3	
Ownership of dwellings	5.8	
Services (including public utilities)	51.3	
B. Services	**51.3**	**100.0**
Public utilities	2.6	5.1
Transportation	7.5	14.7
Railways	0.3	0.7
Road passenger transport	2.2	4.3
Road haulage	1.8	3.4
Shipping	1.8	3.5
Aviation	0.5	1.0
PTT	0.9	1.8
Commerce	14.9	29.0
Trade	11.2	21.8
Banking	2.2	4.4
Insurance	1.5	2.8
Public services	21.0	40.9
General government	9.5	18.4
Central government [c]	7.6	14.7
Local authorities	1.2	2.4
National institutions	0.7	1.3
Other public services	11.5	22.5
Education	4.0	7.8
Health	3.9	7.7
Welfare	0.7	1.4
Business services	1.6	3.1
Other community services [d]	1.3	2.5
Personal services	5.3	10.3
Recreation	0.9	1.6
Domestic services	0.6	1.2
Catering	1.8	3.6
Kibbutzim	1.2	2.4
Personal services n.e.s. [e]	0.8	1.5

Notes to Table 2.1

[a] The branch descriptions in these and subsequent tables have been shortened. See Appendix A for fuller item descriptions.
[b] Before adjustment for depreciation, inventory valuation and public sector interest.
[c] Includes trade organizations (see Appendix A).
[d] Mainly religious institutions.
[e] Mainly laundries and barbers.

SOURCE: CBS, *Israel's National Income and Expenditure (1950–1962)*, Special Series No. 153, 1964. This source is subsequently referred to as NAD (National Accounts Division of the CBS).
For adjustment of the source figures see Appendix B.

TABLE 2.2 *Employed Persons:*[a] *1961*

	Jews		Total		Jews		Non-Jews
	(1)	(2)	(3)	(4)	(5)	(6) [b]	(7) [b]
	thousands				per cent [c]		
A. Total	656.3	687.7	100.0	100.0	100.0	100.0	100.0
Agriculture	76.0	99.4	14.1	11.9	14.5	12.8	41.5
Industry	160.8	168.7	24.6	25.3	24.6	28.2	17.9
Construction	53.0	58.7	8.8	8.3	8.5	10.9	16.1
Services	346.9	359.9	52.5	54.5	52.4	48.1	24.5
Branch not known	19.6	1.0					
B. Services	346.9	359.9	52.5	54.5	52.4	48.1	24.5
Public utilities	13.6	12.8	2.0	2.1	1.9	2.7	0.9
Transportation	42.3	45.7	6.5	6.7	6.7	8.0	4.6
Commerce	80.8	84.7	12.3	12.7	12.3	12.4	7.2
Public services	163.4	165.7	24.6	25.7	24.1	21.1	8.6
Personal services	46.8	51.0	7.1	7.3	7.4	3.9	3.2
C. Total in thousands [d]			709.8	656.3	687.7	483.3	45.8

[a] Census of Population and Housing, June 1961 [columns (1), (3), (4), (6) and (7)]; and Labour Force Surveys (LFS)—annual average [columns (2) and (5)].
[b] Columns (6) and (7) refer to men only.
[c] Per cent calculations in this and subsequent tables exclude 'branch not known.'
[d] Absolute totals in this and subsequent tables include 'not known.'
SOURCE: CBS, *Labour Force Part I*, Census 1961 Publication No. 9, 1963:
Census figures—p. 94, Table 28.
LFS figures—p. 98, Table 31.

TABLE 2.3   *Jewish Employed Persons in Services* [a] *1961*

	Thousands		Per cent of			
			Total		Services	
	Census	LFS	Census	LFS	Census	LFS
All services	**346.9**	**359.9**	**54.5**	**52.4**	**100.0**	**100.0**
Public utilities	**13.6**	**12.8**	**2.1**	**1.9**	**3.9**	**3.6**
Transportation	**42.3**	**45.7**	**6.7**	**6.7**	**12.2**	**12.7**
Railways	2.0	1.8	0.3	0.3	0.6	0.5
Road passenger transport	9.8	9.5	1.6	1.4	2.8	2.6
Road haulage	10.0	13.3	1.6	1.9	2.9	3.7
Shipping	6.9	6.8	1.1	1.0	2.0	1.9
Aviation	2.1	1.8	0.3	0.3	0.6	0.5
PTT	5.8	8.6	0.9	1.2	1.7	2.4
Other transportation	5.7	3.9	0.9	0.6	1.6	1.1
Commerce	**80.8**	**84.7**	**12.7**	**12.3**	**23.3**	**23.5**
Trade	63.1	69.0	9.9	10.0	18.2	19.2
Wholesale trade	*14.5*	*13.3*	*2.3*	*1.9*	*4.2*	*3.7*
Retail trade	*48.6*	*55.7*	*7.6*	*8.1*	*14.0*	*15.5*
Banking	11.5	10.2	1.8	1.5	3.3	2.8
Insurance	6.2	5.5	1.0	0.8	1.8	1.5
Public services	**163.4**	**165.7**	**25.7**	**24.1**	**47.1**	**46.0**
General government	65.7	58.8	10.3	8.5	18.9	16.3
Central government	*43.3*	*41.5*	*6.8*	*6.0*	*12.5*	*11.5*
Local authorities	*10.6*	*7.0*	*1.7*	*1.0*	*3.0*	*1.9*
National institutions	*5.0*	*4.3*	*0.8*	*0.6*	*1.4*	*1.2*
Trade organizations	*6.8*	*6.0*	*1.0*	*0.9*	*2.0*	*1.7*
Other public services	97.7	106.9	15.4	15.6	28.2	29.7
Education	*45.6*	*51.8*	*7.2*	*7.5*	*13.2*	*14.4*
Health	*27.9*	*32.0*	*4.4*	*4.7*	*8.0*	*8.9*
Welfare	*5.4*	*6.0*	*0.9*	*0.9*	*1.6*	*1.7*
Religious institutions	*1.5*	*1.9*	*0.2*	*0.3*	*0.4*	*0.5*
Business services	*11.0*	*10.1*	*1.7*	*1.5*	*3.2*	*2.8*
Other community services	*6.3*	*5.1*	*1.0*	*0.7*	*1.8*	*1.4*

Table 2.3 (cont.)

| | Thousands | | Per cent of | | | |
| | | | Total | | Services | |
	Census	LFS	Census	LFS	Census	LFS
Personal services	**46.8**	**51.0**	**7.3**	**7.4**	**13.5**	**14.2**
Recreation	4.1	3.9	0.6	0.6	1.2	1.1
Domestic services	15.6	19.3	2.4	2.8	4.5	5.4
Restaurants	13.0	13.9	2.0	2.0	3.8	3.9
Hotels	4.9	4.3	0.8	0.6	1.4	1.2
Laundries	3.6	4.4	0.6	0.6	1.0	1.2
Barbers	4.2	4.1	0.7	0.6	1.2	1.1
Other personal services	1.4	1.1	0.2	0.2	0.4	0.3

ª See Table 2.2, note a.
SOURCE: Census data: CBS, *Labour Force Part I, op. cit.,* pp. 108 ff., Table 32. Survey data: Table 2.2 source, and unpublished CBS details.

part corresponds to that of urban housewives, and their income corresponds to the income of housewives; the conventional definitions of labour force and national income exclude such persons and make no imputation for their incomes. [4]

The product-worker ratio

Table 2.4 gives the 1961 product-worker ratio, by branch and sub-branch. In order to calculate the table it was necessary to reconcile as far as possible the domestic product and the labour force coverage. [5] Since the domestic product data are for the whole economy, the figures for both Jewish and non-Jewish employed persons were used. Two adjustments were made to product: (1) the item ownership of dwellings, which consists almost entirely of returns to capital, was excluded (see p. 10), and (2) only that part of product originating in civilian activity was taken into account. The conventional procedure of including ownership of dwellings and non-civilian activities results in an overstatement of the ratio for services.

Table 2.4 uses both the Census and the LFS employment data. The

[4] For figures excluding kibbutz services, see p. 88, Table 4.6.
[5] See also the classification divergences mentioned in the preceding sections.

TABLE 2.4   *The Product-Worker Ratio: 1961*

| | Employed persons | | NDP[a] | Product-worker ratio[b] | |
| | Census | LFS | | (3) ÷ (1) | (3) ÷ (2) |
	(1)	(2)	(3)	(4)	(5)
A. *Total*	**100.0**	**100.0**	**100.0**	1.00	1.00
Agriculture	14.1	17.1	12.1	0.86	0.70
Industry	24.6	23.8	27.4	1.11	1.15
Construction	8.8	9.1	8.2	0.93	0.90
Services (including public utilities)	52.5	50.0	52.3	1.00	1.05
B. *Services*	**52.5**	**50.0**	**52.3**	1.00	1.05
Public utilities	*2.0*	*1.8*	*2.9*	1.42	1.64
Transportation	*6.5*	*6.4*	*8.4*	1.30	1.31
Commerce	*12.3*	*11.9*	*16.5*	1.35	1.39
Trade	9.7	9.7	12.4	1.29	1.29
Banking	1.7	1.4	2.5	1.46	1.73
Insurance	0.9	0.8	1.6	1.73	2.06
Public services	*24.6*	*22.8*	*18.6*	0.76	0.82
General government	9.8	8.0	5.8	0.59	0.73
Other public services	14.8	14.8	12.8	0.87	0.87
Education	7.0	7.2	4.4	0.64	0.62
Health	4.1	4.4	4.4	1.05	0.99
Welfare	0.8	0.8	0.8	0.99	0.95
Business services	1.7	1.4	1.8	1.08	1.28
Other community services	1.2	1.0	1.4	1.15	1.45
Personal services	*7.1*	*7.1*	*5.9*	0.83	0.83
Domestic services	2.3	2.7	0.7	0.29	0.25
Other personal services	4.8	4.4	5.2	1.09	1.18

[a] Adjusted to fit coverage of labour force figures, and excluding ownership of dwellings.
[b] Calculated from less rounded figures underlying the table.
SOURCE: See sources to Tables 2.1 and 2.2.

census gives a lower product-worker ratio than the LFS for 'all services' and for most of the sub-branches. In 'all services' the ratio is equal to the average (i.e., unity) according to the census; for the other branches we have below-average ratios for agriculture and construction, and a considerably above-average ratio in industry. The biggest inter-branch differences occur within services. Distributive services and finance have the highest ratio with banking and insurance leading, followed by transportation and trade. [6] Public and personal services have a ratio of less than unity, as do the sub-branches of the two groups, except for business services and the two heterogeneous 'other' sub-branches.

Some comment is in order: in deriving the ratios for the Jewish sector, the share of the minorities in product and labour force must be taken into account. The concentration of Arabs in agriculture (see Table 2.2), and the fact that product per employed person is usually lower for non-Jews than for Jews, result in a downward bias in agriculture (and construction) and some upward bias in all other branches.

The domestic product figures have not been adjusted for stock valuation and depreciation, and this results in an overestimate of the ratio for the 'productive' branches, in particular, it seems, industry. In the other branches, the adjustments would raise the ratio.

The principal problem derives from the definition of product originating in public sector services—a definition which scarcely takes account of profit or capital services. This makes the absolute level of the ratio for these services largely meaningless. Nevertheless, the very low ratio in general government and public services means that, at least from this point of view, there is nothing to indicate any serious exaggeration of wage-rates in the sector. When a crude estimate of the sector's capital services is taken into account, the conclusion is not altered.[7]

To summarize: we see that in 1961 services accounted for about half of the country's civilian economic activity, both in terms of employment and of product, and that the product-worker ratio for services is close

---

[6] The figure for public utilities is probably not reliable.

[7] This can be illustrated in figures: assume that the 18.6 per cent of product which originates in public services includes 1 per cent returns to capital. Assume also that returns to capital should come to 25 per cent of product originating in the branch. Under the latter assumption, the product originating in the branch will come to 22.4 per cent of total, and the resulting product-worker ratio will be 0.98 and 0.91 according to the LFS and the Census respectively. If, alternatively, we assume that the sector operates at a loss, wage rates may be called excessive from the economic viewpoint, but not as compared with the level in the rest of the economy.

to the country average, although there are considerable inter-branch differences.

2. THE MAIN INTERNATIONAL FINDINGS

The first criterion applied to the data presented in the previous section is the 'level of development.' Per capita national income is commonly accepted as a fairly good reflection of this somewhat vague concept, and it is the measure used in this chapter. The connexion betwen industrial structure and economic development has been the subject of a long line of studies, the more recent of which have stressed also the role of services. In particular, Kuznets' studies (part of a more comprehensive series [8]) devote most of the discussion to problems of the development of services; Colin Clark's book [9] also deals with the subject. We compare our 1961 data for Israel with data for other countries, and try to discover whether Israel's economic structure—in particular the share of services—differs from the international norm and if so, how it differs. The criterion of normality is the level of per capita national income. [10] In the following chapters we shall attempt to explain any divergences found in terms of features peculiar to Israel.

The principal fact to emerge from the studies of Kuznets, Clark, and others, is that there is a connexion—or rather a system of connexions— between per capita national income and industrial structure; this has been found both in an international cross-section and in time series of single countries. There are, however, other factors affecting economic structure in various ways, and not necessarily connected with level of development, or, though connected, not reflected by the income level. This point is discussed by Stigler, who argues that per capita national income represents the principal factors influencing industrial structure

---

[8] S. Kuznets, "Quantitative Aspects of the Economic Growth of Nations, II. Industrial Distribution of National Product and Labor Force," *Economic Development and Cultural Change,* supplement to Vol. V, No. 4, July 1957; and "Quantitative Aspects of the Economic Growth of Nations, III. Industrial Distribution of Income and Labor Force by States, United States 1919–1921 to 1955," *Economic Development and Cultural Change,* Vol. VI, No. 4 Part II, July 1958. The first will be cited as *Countries,* and the second as *States.*

[9] Colin Clark, *The Conditions of Economic Progress* (third edition), London, 1957.

[10] We shall sometimes shorten this to 'income-level.' The words norm, normal, etc. are throughout to be understood in the sense 'found for a given income-level.'

(especially as regards services), but that the correspondence is never uniform or complete. Stigler lists several other factors which directly affect the share of services: the processes of urbanization and specialization, technological change, rising educational standards, a trend to greater equality of income distribution, and the aging of the population. [11] A glance at this list shows that these are in fact concomitants of a growing per capita income. However, development patterns, and the degree of correlation between the various factors and income level, may vary from one country to another; clearly, this implies variations also in patterns of services development. This is a fair criticism of the identification of level of development with per capita income, or of the argument that industrial structure is a function of level of development. Nevertheless, we use the income-level criterion in this chapter; other aspects of development-level will, in so far as they are relevant, be discussed in later chapters.

A further assumption usually made in this type of research is that per capita income is the independent variable, changes in industrial structure being brought about by changes in per capita income. [12] This proposition has been tested by Kuznets, who has shown that differences between developed and undeveloped countries in national product per worker in fact do stem mainly from the general level of productivity, and owe very little to industrial structure.[13] In several of our analyses we shall make explicit use of this assumption.

The several studies of the connexion between per capita national income and economic structure have shown very similar results, and have explained these results in similar ways. This is true both when the researches of different investigators are compared, and when comparing cross-sections with time-series. Table 2.5 gives a brief summary of Kuznets' cross-section findings, and the following paragraphs give a more comprehensive outline of this and the time-series. [14]

[11] G.J. Stigler, *Trends in Employment in the Service Industries*, NBER, Princeton 1956, pp. 160–66.

[12] As Colin Clark (*op. cit.*, p. 493), puts it: "The problem is, how the distribution of Labour Force between these three fields [agriculture, industry, and services] will be affected by increasing real income per head ..."

[13] S. Kuznets, *Countries*, pp. 50–52.
On the other hand, it was found in a time-series study that in several countries changes in industrial structure in themselves contributed to the rise in per capita income. See *ibid*, pp. 52–55.

[14] A concise and comprehensive treatment of the principal features to emerge from the studies may be found in: S. Kuznets, *Six Lectures in Economic*

TABLE 2.5   *The Share of Services by Income-Level Group*
              International Cross-Section: circa 1950[a]

Income level group [b]	I	II	III [c]	IV	V	VI	VII
A. *Per capita national product*							
(index, group VII = 100[b])	1,700	1,000	650	400	270	200	100
B. *The product-share (per cent)*[d]							
S [e]	48.7	41.2	51.6	45.7	40.2	39.3	33.3
T+C	23.6	22.3	21.6	23.4	21.4	15.9	17.6
T	9.5	9.9	8.4	6.7	8.2	4.4	3.3
C	14.1	12.7	14.3	16.7	13.5	12.1	14.4
OS	26.6	18.9	30.0	22.3	20.4	23.4	15.7
C. *The employment-share (per cent)*[d]							
1. Including unpaid family labour [f]							
S [e]	44.8	37.9	42.4	23.7	26.6	20.2	13.5
T+C	23.3	17.8	16.9	9.4	10.4	7.7	6.9
T	8.4	6.8	6.0	3.3	3.2	2.5	2.3
C	14.9	11.0	10.9	6.1	7.4	5.2	4.6
OS	21.6	20.2	25.5	14.2	13.7	12.5	6.5
2. Excluding unpaid family labour [f]							
S [e]	45.3	41.7	41.8	28.2	28.3	26.1	23.7
T+C	23.7	18.9	17.8	12.0	12.1	9.6	8.3
T	8.6	7.6	6.4	4.0	4.0	3.5	2.6
C	15.1	11.4	11.5	8.0	8.2	6.1	5.8
OS	21.7	22.8	24.0	16.2	16.2	16.6	15.3
D. *The product-worker ratio* [g]							
1. Including unpaid family labour [f]							
S [e]	1.04	1.12	1.23	2.38[h]	1.57	2.10	2.79
T+C	0.98	1.20	1.28	4.08[h]	2.07	2.58	3.75
OS	1.24	1.02	1.20	1.73[h]	1.50	2.09	2.63
2. Excluding unpaid family labour [f]							
S [e]	1.02	0.98	1.19	1.54	1.39	1.60	1.52
T+C	0.97	1.11	1.23	2.04	1.83	1.90	1.82
OS	1.26	0.85	1.17	1.16	1.25	1.52	1.39

[a] The dates vary from country to country. See the Appendix Tables in the source.
[b] The seven groups are those of Kuznets (see Source). The average for group VII is $ 60–$ 70.
[c] Israel is included in the group III data (except in Panels C.2 and D.2—see note f). The figures are for the early years of the State; their inclusion is one of the causes of the out-of-line behaviour of group III, in both product and employment shares.
[d] Unweighted arithmetic means of the product and employment shares of the

Notes to Table 2.5 (cont.)

    countries in each income group.
ᵉ Figures for subsectors do not necessarily add to the total, since subsector detail
  was not always available for all countries surveyed. The symbols stand for:

S—all services

T—transportation and public utilities

C—commerce

OS—other services

  In the product-share figures, the C sector includes only trade, and finance is
  included in OS.
  The product-share of ownership of dwellings is in OS. With these exceptions,
  the classification is broadly consistent with that used by us in Section 1 of this
  chapter (see Appendix A).
ᶠ The principal effect of including unpaid family labour is to raise the share
  of agriculture and reduce the share of other sectors in the less developed
  countries. The labour force definitions used in Israel include unpaid family
  labour and we therefore use these figures in our comparisons.
ᵍ Does not necessarily equal Panel B÷Panel C figures, since only countries for
  which there are both product and employment data are included in the
  ratio calculation.
ʰ Turkey, whose ratios are exceptional, is one of 5 countries covered by these
  cells. Without Turkey the ratios are: S—1.69; T+C—2.27; and OS—1.30.
SOURCE: S. Kuznets, *Countries:*

Income-level index—p. 7

Product share—Tables 3 and 6

Employment share—Tables 10 and 13

Product-worker ratio—Tables 18 and 20.

In the cross-section,[15] there is no clear tendency for the share of
product originating in services to rise (or decline) with per capita
income. A positive correlation is found by Kuznets only in the low
income ranges, and it disappears at higher incomes (over the $400
per capita level—Group III countries, see Table 2.5, and p. 23). In
the time series, it was found that the share of product originating in
services rose in half the countries studied and declined in the other
half.[16] In the Clark study, however, a clear positive correlation was
found between the share of product originating in (somewhat differently
defined) services and the income-level. Here, however, the product
share was calculated at constant prices.[17] If the two researches are
comparable, the difference in their findings suggests that the lack of

---

  Growth, The Free Press of Glencoe, Ill., 1959, Lecture III, in particular
pp. 60–67.
[15] S. Kuznets, *Countries,* pp. 13–16.
[16] *Ibid.,* p. 17.
[17] In international units (I.U.). In addition, Clark differs from Kuznets in
  including construction and crafts in services, and in using cross-section and
  historical data at the same time. See C. Clark, *op. cit.,* pp. 377–79.

correlation in the current-price data can be at least partly explained by relative-price movements.

A much higher positive correlation is found between income-level and the employment share of services. It is for this reason that many investigators have concentrated on the employment rather than the product aspect of the share of services. The correlation was found for both cross-section and time series—more strongly for the latter.

The inter-country range of variation of both product and employment share was fairly narrow, regardless of whether there was any correlation with income-level.

In all studies the product-worker ratio of services was found to be considerably higher than the all-industry average, and to decline significantly as income rises; however, a few of the time-series countries did not conform to this rule.

That the employment share of services rises with income-level is explained in the literature mainly by two factors: first, and more important, is the steep increase in demand for services (as compared with goods), both for final and intermediate use. Clark, Kuznets, and Stigler single out the increase in the demand of enterprises for intermediate services—an increase stimulated by the process of specialization and the increased complexity of the economic system which accompanied and followed the Industrial Revolution. The second factor is that services generally lag behind agriculture and industry in technological development; this means a relative decline in real output per unit of input (and per labour unit) of services, or a rise in the relative—if not the absolute —amount of labour required to produce a given amount of services. Kuznets explicitly mentions this, while Clark does not altogether agree with him, and Stigler's discussion also shows that he does not accept the hypothesis in its entirety. Nevertheless, there seems to be agreement that the factor plays a part, at some stages of development at least.[18]

---

[18] S. Kuznets, *Countries*, p. 32; C. Clark, *op. cit.*, pp. 494–95; G.J. Stigler, *op. cit.*, pp. 157–59; and S. Fabricant, *Trends in Government Activity Since 1900*, NBER, New York, 1952, pp. 98–102 (in connexion with government services).

Clark explicitly refutes the old argument about the productivity-lag of services, and maintains that most of the rise in services employment is due to increased demand, while "... the efficiency of transport and commerce, in certain stages of a country's economic development, may advance even more rapidly than those of manufactures ..."

Stigler stresses mainly organizational technological improvements in the various service branches.

A third possibility must be explored, namely, that labour is only one of the inputs of services output; in the course of development and technological change there might be substitution between labour and capital. Clearly, some technological changes occurring in services may be more labour-saving than those in other branches. These will reduce the employment share of services even if the level of technological change lags behind that in other branches. On the other hand, capital-saving improvements will tend to raise the services employment share regardless of their intensity. We have no clear evidence of the nature of techno- logical change in services, but what there is suggests that even if improvements in services are in themselves labour-saving and capital- consuming, the improvements in other branches are often even more so; in effect, therefore, technological change in services is relatively labour-consuming and capital-saving. [19]

Demand for services such as domestic, religious, and some personal services declines as per capita income rises, while the demand for most services grows; this is the chief explanation of the small range of vari- ation of the services employment share—small when compared with other branches, especially agriculture. Moreover, in many countries labour concentrates in services in the early stages of development; this is because workers leaving agriculture cannot find better-paid work, owing to the shortage of capital and to the competition in the industrial product market of more advanced countries; petty trade, various per- sonal services and even government may be affected. [20]

The explanations advanced for the relatively narrow range of vari- ation in the employment share of services hold good also for the product share. Here, the dispersion was even narrower, and there was, moreover, no correlation with income-level. Two explanations of this divergence from the employment findings may be offered:

a. The lag in relative labour-productivity in services as the economy develops (see p. 20). If there is such a lag, labour input will rise more than real services output, as the relative demand for services rises.

b. Changes in the relative price of services as the economy develops.

---

[19] In many services fixed capital cannot be exploited in three shifts, but at most for one or occasionally two shifts (most professional services, education, health, government, personal services, banking, trade, etc.). This problem is discussed by P.T. Bauer and B.S. Yamey, "Economic Progress and Occupational Distribution" in *The Economic Journal*, December 1951, pp. 741–55.

[20] S. Kuznets, *Countries*, pp. 14–16, and G.J. Stigler, *op. cit.*, p. 165. In Chapter 5 we shall return to the problem of services overconcentration at early stages of development.

The increased demand and the productivity-lag operate to raise the relative price of services, and should have led to a clear rise in their product-share. However, at certain stages of growth, there is apparently a third, offsetting, factor at work. This is the decline in the money incomes per unit of output of services workers, which stems from the decline in the economic-rent element in these incomes. Kuznets, Clark, and others explain this phenomenon by the increased pool of labour suitable for service occupations owing to the rise in the standard of education, and its spread to the whole population; by the breaking of the monopolistic position of small groups in trade, finance and foreign trading—monopolies which had their origin in the shortage of suitable labour and in the social and political system; and by the process of urbanization which brought a supply of labour to the (geographical) centres of demand for services. The decline in the services product share is not typical of all countries, periods, and services, and there are plenty of instances where the product share rose, sometimes even more than the employment share. [21]

Clearly, the result of the interplay of these forces—increased demand, productivity lag, and decline in the economic rent element of service workers' incomes—will, *a priori,* depend on the intensity of each.

The various studies stress the great variety of behaviour found in different service branches, and in some of them the connexion with income level is in the opposite direction to that of most services.

In both time-series and cross-section studies there was a positive correlation between income-level and the employment share (in descending order) in: transportation, commerce, 'other services'. In the historical study, this does not hold for transport in the states of the USA, where a negative correlation was found, and there are similar findings in Colin Clark. Within 'other services', the US studies show that the employment share of domestic services [22] declined as income-level rose, while for most of the other components of the group the employment share rose.

No systematic connexion can be found between income level and the product share even when the service industries are taken separately; in fact, the different studies and investigators do not always agree. The exceptions are transportation in the Kuznets international study, and

[21] See below.

[22] G. J. Stigler, *op. cit.,* p. 7, Table 4. The Kuznets studies show that with rising per capita income the employment share of domestic services declines at first, but begins to rise moderately at the higher income levels. For this and related matters see S. Kuznets, *States,* pp. 62–65.

finance and several private services (catering and entertainment, liberal professions) in the study of American states: in these branches the product share rose.

The product-worker ratios of commerce and transportation are above the all-industry average, even in advanced countries and after a long-term decline; in some of the other branches, the product-worker ratio declines to less than unity. At all income levels the ranking of service industries by product-worker ratio is as follows: finance, trade, transportation, and 'other services', within the last, the ratio is highest for liberal professions, and lowest for domestic services.

3. ISRAEL AND OTHER COUNTRIES

All services

In order to examine the connexion between industrial structure and income level, Kuznets divided the countries (or states, in the US inter-state comparison) into income groups, and calculated unweighted arithmetic averages of the indicators he wished to compare (employment share of services, etc.). We shall call this the group-average method. A second method, and the one followed by us, is to attempt to fit a simple linear relationship to the indicator examined: we calculated the regression of the various magnitudes on per capita income for various countries, and where significant results were obtained, the Israel figure was compared to that predicted by the regression line; this will be referred to as the regression method. The use of the least-squares method in the treatment of this problem has many drawbacks, and use will therefore be made of this method only when the results bear some resemblance to the result of other ways of comparison, in particular of the group averages method. A third method, the comparison of isolated points from other countries and periods, was used when there were not enough data for any of the other methods. In our discussion of each branch, we shall deal first with employment shares since they are connected more strongly than product shares with income level.

In 1961 the per capita income of Israel was $ 627 (at the exchange rate of IL 3/$ 1 introduced by the devaluation of February 1962.[23])

[23] In 1961, national income was IL 4,119 million [CBS, *Statistical Bulletin of Israel*, Part B, Economic Statistics, May 1963 (Hebrew)]. Although IL 2.5/$1 is probably a more realistic exchange rate for 1691, we have used IL 3/$1 because the international data of our comparison use $ of the early 1950's, when the US dollar was worth about 20 percent more in terms of its own purchasing power than in 1961.

TABLE 2.6   *The Share of Services: Israel Compared with Other Countries*

	Israel 1961 [a]		Income-group averages		Regression [b]		
	L F S	Census	II	I	All Countries [c]	Group I–III Countries [c]	States (1950)

A. Product share (per cent)

S [d]		57.1	41.2	48.7			
T+C		21.3	22.3	23.6			
T [e]		10.1	9.9	9.5			
C		14.9					
Trade		*11.2*	*12.7*	*14.1*			
Finance		*3.7*	*(2.4)*	*(3.1)*			
OS		32.1					
OS including finance		35.8	18.9	26.6			

B. Employment share (per cent)

S [d]	50.0	52.5	37.9	44.8	36.3		45.5
T+C	20.1	20.8	17.8	23.3	17.0 [f]		22.7 [g]
T [e]	8.2	8.5	6.8	8.4	6.1		5.7
C	11.9	12.3	11.0	14.9	10.9		16.9 [g]
Trade	*9.7*	*9.7*	..	..	..		..
Finance	*2.2*	*2.6*	..	..	..		..
OS	29.9	31.7	20.2	21.6	19.5		[h]

C. Product-worker ratio [i]

S [d]	1.11	1.05	1.12	1.04	1.37	1.14	
T+C excluding finance product			1.20	0.98	1.63	1.20	
T+C	1.30	1.26	(1.28)	(1.11)			
T	1.30	1.25	..	..			
C	1.31	1.26	..	..			
Trade	1.21	1.21	..	..			
OS	0.97	0.92	(0.94)	(1.09)			
OS including finance product			1.02	1.24			

[a] Jews and non-Jews.
[b] The predictions are for a per capita income of $ 627 (i.e., somewhat less than the $ 670 average income for group II).
[c] Various dates round 1950 (see note a to Table 2.5).
[d] Symbols and classification are explained in note e to Table 2.5.

Notes to Table 2.6 (cont.)

[e] We have made a crude attempt to split the T sector into transportation and public utilities:

	Israel	*I*	*II*	*V—VII*	*IV, III*
1. Employment-share (per cent)					
a. Number of countries					
in calculation		6	6	6	8
b. Transportation	6.4–6.5	7.5	6.1	4.6	2.5
c. Public utilities	1.8–2.0	1.2	0.6	0.8	0.3
2. Product-share (per cent)					
a. Number of countries		5		7	7
b. Public utilities	2.6	1.9		0.5	0.6

[f] The sum of the results for T and C.
[g] Includes restaurants and cafes—about 3 per cent.
[h] No correlation was found.
[i] An attempt was made to adjust the Kuznets data for the classification divergence between product and employment, by shifting 2.4 per cent and 3.1 per cent (respectively, groups I and II) product-share from OS to T+C. The results are shown in parentheses. The group I figure for OS (4 countries) is affected by the exceptionally high figure for Belgium; the average for the other three countries is 0.94.

SOURCE: Israel—product share, Table 2.1; employment share, Table 2.4.
  Country income group averages, Table 2.5.
  Regression—Countries: Figures for Philippines, Guatemala, Greece, Panama, Colombia, Cuba and Malaya from ILO, *Yearbook of Labour Statistics 1961*, Table 6; other countries, S. Kuznets, *Countries*, Appendix Table 3 (for employment share). *Ibid.*, Appendix Tables 1 and 5 (for product share and product-worker ratio).
  States: S. Kuznets, *States*, Appendix Table 14.
  In addition to these sources, note e draws on UN, *Demographic Yearbook 1955*, and UN, *Statistics of National Income and Expenditure*, Series H, No. 10.

Table 2.6 summarizes the principal comparisons between industrial structure in Israel and other countries, for all services together, and for each of the main services. The data relate to 1961 for Israel, 1948–53 for the countries, and 1950 for the American states.[24]

All the income-level comparisons show that in Israel the employment share of services is considerably above the international norm. In Israel 52.5 per cent and 50 per cent (according to the Census of Population and the LFS, respectively) of the labour force were employed in services, compared with 37.9 per cent in the relevant group of countries, 36.2 ($\pm$1.4) per cent predicted by the regression for all countries, and the 45.5 ($\pm$1.9) per cent predicted by the regression for the American states. [25]

[24] We shall, somewhat loosely, refer to 'countries' and 'states' in this connexion.
[25] The regression lines obtained were as follows:

  I. 46 countries: $L_{S_1} = 22 \cdot 10^{-3}x + 22.2$, $r = 0.72$;
  $(32 \cdot 10^{-4})$

Further, the figure for Israel is above the average for the group I countries, and equals that in the richest countries of the group. [26] In most of the countries, the figure for services employment also includes the armed forces. Non-civilian employees add another 2 to 3 percentage points to the Israel figure.[27] There is some justification for not including the armed forces, since the defence burden—both in terms of outlay and manpower—is itself above normal.[28] Be that as it may, the services employment-share in Israel is 12 to 16 percentage points above the normal level, a relative difference of over 30 per cent. This is considerable in a sector whose range of variation is relatively narrow and where few countries depart so far from the norm. [29]

In the absence of a clear correlation between income level and the services product share, there is no point in using the income level criterion for the product share comparison. We saw (in Table 2.5) that the highest services product share was found in group III (per capita income of $ 400 to $ 450).

Nevertheless, the data show that the Israel figures are higher than those in most other countries, regardless of income-level. The services

---

$$\text{and } L_{S_2} = 25.4 \log x - 31.5, \qquad\qquad r = 0.80$$
$$(2.9)$$

where L_S is the employment share in 'all services' and x is the per capita national income. The prediction for $ 627 from log income is 39.6 ($\pm$ 1.4) per cent.

II. 48 American states: $L_{S_3} = 99 \cdot 10^{-4} x + 39.2,$ $r = 0.44$
$$(29 \cdot 10^{-4})$$

(significant for this number of cases).

The figures in parentheses in the text are the standard errors of the predictions, and in the footnote, the standard errors of the regression coefficients. The states all fall roughly into the group I income level; thus, their lower regression coefficient perhaps indicates that the rise in L_S is more moderate at higher incomes, and hence also that the normal estimate is too high for Israel's income level.

[26] The figure is higher only in the US (53.1 per cent). Australia has 49.2 per cent; New Zealand, 48.1 per cent; Argentina, 46.9 per cent; Canada, 46.6 per cent; UK, 47.5 per cent; and the Netherlands, 47.4 per cent. (S. Kuznets, *Countries*, Appendix Table 3).

[27] According to A. Hovne, *The Labor Force in Israel*, FP, July 1961, p. 17.

[28] In 1950, the proportion of the employed labour force in the armed forces was 2 per cent in the US (G.J. Stigler, *op. cit.*, pp. 3 and 6) and 3 per cent in Great Britain (M. Abramovitz and V.F. Eliasberg, *The Growth of Public Employment in Great Britain*, NBER, Princeton, 1957, p. 25, Table 1.

[29] See Table 3.4, p. 52.

product-share in Israel is 57 per cent,—one of the highest in the world. [30]

The Israel product-worker ratio is 1.05 (Census data) and 1.11 (LFS). The figure for the relevant country group is 1.12 or the same as the Israel LFS figure. [31]

The correlation coefficients for income level and product-worker ratio were significant both for the whole S sector, and for T+C and OS. However, a straight line does not give a good prediction, so that we could not get a significant estimate of the normal product-worker ratio. The data for countries of income groups I to III, for which a linear regression seems more plausible, gave correlation coefficients which were not significant at the 5 per cent level; however, the predictions obtained for $ 627 per capita income were very close to the group II averages. [32] We shall therefore confine our discussion of product-worker ratio to the group averages method.

In the other industries we obtained the following results: the share of agriculture in Israel is fairly similar to that of group I countries, whether in terms of employment, product or the product-worker ratio; the last two indicators are in Israel somewhat lower than for group I, but if we were to include only the Jewish sector in the comparison, the resemblance would be much closer. [33]

[30] Higher figures are found only in Puerto Rico (63.6 per cent) and the Lebanon (64.1 per cent); in Egypt, Jamaica, Mexico, Chile, and the US, the level is similar. (Kuznets, *Countries,* Appendix Table 1.)

The Israel figure here includes the product of ownership of dwellings in addition to services as defined in Section 1 of this chapter, since this is as a rule the procedure in the international data of our comparison.

[31] The product-worker ratio for Israel is not the same as that shown in Table 2.4 as ownership of dwellings is included in product (see note 30 above).

In the Kuznets data, which refer to the years around 1950, Israel is in group III. By 1961, however, Israel's per capita income was about $ 625, so that group II is here the 'relevant group'. (Table 2.5, Panel D.1.)

[32] The predictions are: RP_1 (627) = 1.14, for S; and RP_3 (627) = 1.20, for T + C.

[33] The figures for agriculture are:

Employment share: Israel (LFS)—17 per cent; Jews only—14.5 per cent; group I countries—15 per cent.

Product-share: Israel—10.9 per cent; group I—13.2 per cent.

Product-worker ratio: Israel—0.66; group I—0.86; (the figure for Jews in Israel is some 5 to 6 per cent higher).

These data are from our worksheets, and from Kuznets, *Countries,* Tables 3, 10, and 16.

The Kuznets data combine all other branches in one sector (M), which covers manufacturing, crafts, quarrying, and construction. The employment-share of this sector in Israel is close to that in group II countries. The product share for Israel is close to the group III figure (Israel 32.0 per cent; group III, 29.2 per cent). The product-worker ratio is 1.01 in Israel and 1.03 for groups I and III. It should be noted that in sector M neither product-share nor product-worker ratio are strongly correlated with per capita income.

We see that in terms of the employment share of services (and even in agriculture) Israel is similar to a group of richer countries; but the high product share is not enough to lift the product-worker ratio above that of the comparable income-level group. We shall now examine how far these findings hold good for the services separately.

Transportation and public utilities

For purposes of comparison we follow Kuznets in combining trans-portation with public utilities. The rationale of the combination is that public utilities are primarily concerned with the distribution of water and electricity to consumers, even when regular forms of transportation are not involved. In 1961, 8.2 per cent of employed labour force in Israel was in this group, 6.5 per cent in transportation. This is higher than the figure for the comparable income-group. The relevant group average is 6.8 per cent (Table 2.5), and the figure obtained from the regression is 6.1 ($\pm$ 0.3) per cent. [34] The prediction made from the regression for the American states (1950) is even lower—5.69 ($\pm$0.59) per cent. [35] Despite doubts as to whether the data are uniformly defined, it seems that for the T sector, as for S as a whole, Israel resembles the richest group of countries (where the figure is 8.4 per cent). In other words, some, but not all, of Israel's excess services employment is in transportation and public utilities. Data for transportation and public utilities separately were found for a few countries (note e to Table 2.6). They suggest that most of the excess is in public utilities, rather than in transportation. The international public utilities employment figures

[34] $L_{T_1} = 55 \cdot 10^{-4}x + 2.7;$ $r = 0.74.$
      $(77 \cdot 10^{-5})$

[35] $L_{T_3} = 26 \cdot 10^{-4}x + 4.1;$ $r = 0.77.$
      $(32 \cdot 10^{-5})$

This does not differ significantly from the countries regression. Although time-series findings show that the employment share of the sector declines as a higher income-level is reached, cross-section studies show a positive correla-tion with employment share at all income levels.

are not very reliable, because the heading covers different branches in different countries; we shall therefore not analyse the findings for this branch. The group averages for transportation were 6.1. per cent in group II countries, compared with about 6.5 per cent for Israel and 7.5 per cent for group I.

The T sector is the only one for which there was a significant positive correlation ($r = 0.51$) between income level and product share.[36] The group averages series also shows the same picture (Table 2.5), so that we can here speak of a normal product share. This normal share is 9.9 per cent (group II average) and 8.0 (± 0.7) per cent according to the regression (for all countries). The corresponding figure for Israel is 10 per cent; this is higher than for most countries of Israel's income group, and higher than for some group I countries.[37] The data for a small number of countries (Table 2.6, note e) suggest that the product share of transportation (without public utilities) comes to about 8 per cent in group I and II countries; this is fairly close to the Israel figure. As with the employment share the principal difference is thus in public utilities; the data are, however, highly dubious.

The Kuznets study gives no estimates of the product-worker ratio for the T sector alone, but only figures combined with trade (T+C). This makes the comparison very difficult. Some of Clark's figures, the Kuznets data on the American states, and crude calculations made by us from the Kuznets countries data suggest that the product-worker ratio for the T sector in Israel is at any rate no lower than normal.[38]

---

[36] $Y_T = 40 \cdot 10^{-4}x + 5.4,$
    $(11 \cdot 10^{-4})$
where Y_T is the per cent of product originating in the T sector.

[37] The group II average is raised by the high figure (14.6 per cent) for maritime Norway, the figures for other countries in the group being 11 per cent or less.

[38] See Colin Clark, op. cit., p. 522 (facing), Table I, and S. Kuznets, States, p. 79, Table 33.
    The Israel figure is 1.26 to 1.30. A similar or higher figure is found by Clark only for Denmark, Canada and South Africa. In the poorest group of states the ratio was 1.52 in 1929 and 1.30 in 1950; at these dates, however, this group had a higher per capita income than Israel in 1961. Since there is a negative correlation with income level, we should have expected, from the 1950 figure, a somewhat higher ratio for Israel. The figures of our own calculation (based on the Kuznets countries data) are 1.35 for group II countries, and 1.07 for group I. (Kuznets, Countries, Appendix Tables 1 and 3.)

Commerce

In Israel, the employment share of finance is around 2.5 per cent, and of trade and finance together (commerce) around 12 per cent (Table 2.6). This only slightly exceeds the findings for other countries according both to group averages (11.0 per cent in group II) and to the regression [10.9 ($\pm$0.4) per cent.] The figure for American states is higher, even allowing for the inclusion of 'restaurants and cafes'.[39] If the Israel figures are in fact higher than the international norm, the excess can apparently be divided between trade and finance. [40]

It should be noted that sector C shows a stronger correlation of income level with employment share than do other services.

The Kuznets countries data on income originating in sector C cover only trade, and not finance, which is included in 'other services.' [41] The product share is fairly constant over all country groups, and varies irregularly in a very narrow range between 12.1 and 14.4 per cent, except for 16.7 per cent in group IV (see Table 2.5, panel B). In Israel, the figure for trade is about 11 per cent; this is somewhat below the lowest average, though well above the figure for a considerable number of single countries. Our data are not sufficiently reliable to enable us to say that this represents a significant deviation from the norm. For finance, Kuznets found a positive correlation between product share

---

[39] Countries: $L_{C_1} = 85 \cdot 10^{-4}x + 5.6$; $r = 0.78$.
$\qquad\qquad\quad (10 \cdot 10^{-4})$

States: $L_{C_2} = 52 \cdot 10^{-4}x + 13.7$; $r = 0.57$.
$\qquad\qquad\quad (11 \cdot 10^{-4})$

The prediction for \$ 627 per capita income is 16.9 ($\pm$ 0.8) per cent.

[40] The employment-share of finance was 3.33 per cent in the US in 1950 (G.J. Stigler, *op. cit.*, p. 7, Table 4) and 2.4 per cent in the UK in 1961 (Central Statistical Office, *Annual Abstract 1962*, HMSO).

Stigler's historical US series suggests that the employment-share of finance is correlated with income level. The Kuznets countries data (quoted in Table 2.5, panel C) show a clear correlation for the whole C sector, as do his data for the states *(States,* p. 64. Table 26). If we accept this evidence, the Israel finance figure (at any rate the 2.6 per cent from the Census data) appears to be above the international norm.

[41] This divergence in the classification of the Kuznets employment and product data may be seen from the principal sources of data: UN, *Statistics of National Income and Expenditure,* Statistical Papers Series H, Nos. 8 and 9 (industrial origin of product), and UN, *Demographic Yearbook 1955* (distribution of labour force).

and income level in the American states. [42] In the poorest group of states the product share is about 3 per cent, and the arithmetic mean for all the states is 3.7 per cent. Data on the product share of finance (in about 30 countries for a date around 1950) show that the group II average is 2.4 per cent, and the group I average is 3.1 per cent. [43] If, as these figures suggest, there is a positive correlation with income level, it can be said that the Israel figure exceeds the norm.

It is difficult to get a common basis for comparison for the product-worker ratio (in either trade or finance). In addition to the fact that Kuznets shows only the combined T+C sector, there is the problem we have already encountered that product originating in finance was included in OS. The Israel product-worker ratio (1.26 to 1.30, both for commerce and for the sector T+C) seems to be higher than the group II figure (1.20, as the group average, and from the regression for groups I–III). However, if we adjust for the product-share of finance, we get a ratio of 1.35, which is somewhat above the Israel figure. [44]

The T+C sector figures are shown in Table 2.6. The employment share in Israel was 2 to 3 per cent above the international norm (both the group II average and according to the regression). The product share of the sector is similar to that of group II countries, but as stated, the finding is not very significant. The product-worker ratio in the sector is somewhat lower (after the appropriate adjustments) than that found for group II. All the component branches deviate from the international norm, but no firm conclusions can be drawn, owing to the small size of each deviation and the poor reliability of our data.

'Other services'

In the available sources, the services employment data for most countries are not shown in detail, and public and personal services are included in the residual item 'other services.' In Israel, the sector employs 30 to 32 per cent of civilian employed persons. The group averages data show a positive correlation between employment share

---

[42] See S. Kuznets, *States*, pp. 34, 37, and Table 14.

[43] The average for group III and IV countries is 2.4 per cent, and for group V–VII countries, 1.5 per cent. The figure exceeds 3 per cent only for Canada, the US, and the Lebanon. See UN, *National Income and Expenditure*, Statistical Papers Series H, No. 10.

[44] The adjustment consisted principally of transferring 2.4 per cent of product from OS to T+C in the group II countries. In the same way we get a product-worker ratio of 1.07 for group I (see the figures in parentheses in Table 2.6, panel C).

and income level except for group III. The regression also shows a
positive correlation. [45] The group II average is 20.2 per cent, and the
regression prediction (for all countries) for $ 627 per capita is 19.3
(± 0.9) per cent. This is clear evidence of overconcentration in 'other
services' in Israel, where the employment share is more than 50 per
cent above the norm.

The product share of 'other services' (including finance and ownership of dwellings) is 35.8 per cent in Israel, and is exceeded only by
Puerto Rico, with 39.3 per cent. The result is so clear that it does not
perhaps matter that no correlation between income-level and product
share was found for the sector. There were no data for 'other services'
excluding finance and ownership of dwellings for the countries in the
Kuznets study; we obtained data on the narrower definition for some
30 countries, and these showed that here too Israel is well ahead with
26 per cent, followed by only a few countries with more than 20 per
cent (Egypt, Jamaica, Chile, South Africa, UK, and US). The Israel
product-share of ownership of dwellings (5.8 per cent) also seems to be
high in comparison with other countries. Although the data are not
sufficient to establish whether there is a correlation with income level,
this figure was not approached in any of the advanced countries except
Belgium. The proportion of owner-occupied dwellings varies widely
from one country to another, as do methods of imputing their product.
This accounts in large measure for the inter-country differences in this
item. [46]

For product-worker ratio, the classification adjustment must be made
(see p. 31, text and note 44). Without adjustment the product-worker
ratio is slightly lower in Israel than in group II, which itself has the
lowest group ratio. After adjustment, the group II figure is about 0.90,
somewhat lower than the Israel figure. If it is remembered that the
group II ratio is lower than that of other groups, and that there is no
strong correlation with income level, it cannot be said that the Israel
ratio for these branches is above the international norm.[47] All the

---

[45] $L_{os} = 84 \cdot 10^{-4}x + 14.0;$ $r = 0.49.$
    $(23 \cdot 10^{-4})$

No correlation was found for the American states.

[46] The data were taken from UN, *Statistics of National Income and Expenditure*,
Series H, No. 10, and are averages for 1950–54. The product concept and
the branch classification used are not always consistent with those of the
earlier publications in the series from which Kuznets derived his data.

[47] However, the product-worker ratio for group I, which represents only four
countries, is affected by the high figure for Belgium (1.55). In the other

calculations so far cited include ownership of dwellings, whose product share is, as stated, rather high in Israel. We may thus conclude that if the item is excluded from the OS sector, the ratio for Israel will be closer to that of group II.

For the other components of the OS sector we have data for only a few countries. In attempting the comparison we concentrate mainly on the employment share.

In the cross-section of American states Kuznets finds the following relationships between employment shares and income level. In the first place, there is a clear positive correlation in personal services. Within personal services, there is also a positive correlation for 'professional services', which on the whole corresponds to 'other public services' in our classification. There is a negative correlation with income level in domestic services in all groups of states except for the richest, where the employment share again rises. [48] If we also use the data on product share by income level, we can add to this finding a positive correlation for 'hotels and entertainment' and 'business services and repairs.' [49]

Table 2.7 compares the labour force distribution in the OS sector in Israel, the United States and Great Britain. It appears that there is no overconcentration in personal services: the Israel employment share for this group is lower than the American figure by about one third. The last item in the table appears to be more broadly defined in the US, but in any case the Israel figures include personal services in kibbutzim, which should not as a rule be included in an international comparison. [50]

In branches whose employment share is positively correlated with income level, there is still a wide margin for expansion in Israel, and there is no reason to suppose that the employment share is higher than

---

three countries the ratio is below the group II average. Without Belgium the group I average is 0.90 (about 0.80 after making the finance adjustment).

[48] S. Kuznets, *States*, p. 64, Table 26, and p. 65.

Our regression for domestic services in the American states gave the following results:

$$L_D = -21 \cdot 10^{-4}x + 5.5; \qquad\qquad r = -0.55.$$
$$(47 \cdot 10^{-5})$$

The figure predicted for Israel's income level is 4.1 ($\pm$ 0.4) per cent.

[49] *Ibid.*, pp. 36–38. In general, the employment share is more strongly correlated with income level than the product share.

[50] See pp. 9, 13. The employment share of kibbutz personal services is 1.5 per cent (Table 4.6).

TABLE 2.7   *Employment in 'Other Services' in the United States, the United Kingdom and Israel*

	United States[a] 1950		United Kingdom, 1961	Israel, 1961 Total population		Jews	
	(a)	(b)		Census	LFS	Census	LFS
A. Total employed civilian labour force— thousands	57,463	56,239	24,464	710	746	656	688
B. Public and personal services—							
per cent of total	**24.3**	**22.7**	**24.0**	**31.7**	**29.9**	**33.0**	**31.5**
Public services	**13.7**	**15.4**	**14.6**	**24.6**	**22.8**	**25.7**	**24.1**
General government	*4.4*	*4.5*	*5.3*	*9.8*	*8.0*	*10.3*	*8.5*
Central government	1.8	..	2.2	6.5		6.8	6.0
Local authorities	1.8[b]	..	3.1	1.6		1.7	1.0
Postal services	0.8	..	–	–		–	–
National institutions[c]	–	–	–	1.7		1.8	1.5
Other public services	*9.3*	*10.9*	*9.3*	*14.8*	*14.8*	*15.4*	*15.6*
Education	3.8			7.0		7.2	7.5
Health	3.1			4.1		4.4	4.7
Welfare, religious and other community services	1.0	8.4		2.0		2.1	1.9
Legal and engineering services	0.7			1.7		1.7	1.5
Business services	0.7[d]	2.5					
Personal services	**10.6**	**7.3**	**9.4**	**7.1**[e]	**7.1**[e]	**7.3**[e]	**7.4**[e]
Recreation	0.9	1.0		0.6		0.6	0.6
Domestic services	2.8	..		2.3		2.4	2.8
Restaurants	3.1[f]	..		2.0		2.0	2.0
Hotels	0.9			0.8		0.8	0.6
Laundries	1.2	6.3[g]		0.6		0.6	0.6
Barbers	0.6			0.6		0.7	0.6
Other personal services	1.1			0.2		0.2	0.2

[a] Estimate (a) is for total labour force and estimate (b) for employed labour force. The differences between the two sources are small. Estimate (a) suggests that Federal postal services are also included in estimate (b).

Federal government health and education employees are allocated to the relevant items in 'other public services'. The armed forces are excluded from the table, as are another 1.8 per cent of labour force employed by government

Notes to Table 2.7 (cont.)

in various activities which should not, in our classification, be included here.
ᵇ Includes state administrations.
ᶜ Includes also trade and professional associations (see Appendix A), which in the other countries are probably included in 'other public services.'
ᵈ Estimate (a) was compiled from scattered tables in the source. Comparison with estimate (b) suggests that some misclassification or omission may have occurred here.
ᵉ According to the Census, employment in personal services of kibbutzim was about 1.3 per cent of total employment: 0.7 per cent in domestic services; 0.6 per cent in 'restaurants' and a negligible amount in the other items.
ᶠ In the official US statistics [and in estimate (b)] this item is included in trade.
ᵍ Includes domestic services.
SOURCE: United States: (a)—Compiled from G. J. Stigler, *op. cit.*
                        (b)—US Bureau of the Census, *Statistical Abstract of the United States, 1956,* p. 209.
        United Kingdom—CSO, *Annual Abstract of Statistics 1961,* HMSO.
        Israel—Tables 2.3 and 2.4.

warranted by Israel's income level. We shall not discuss in detail branches such as domestic services, where the Israel employment share is below that of the same income level group. However, Stigler finds a positive correlation between the employment share of domestic services and the index of inequality of income distribution. If we accept this thesis, the low (compared with the US) Israel figure clearly makes sense. [51]

There is much more overconcentration in public services. Here, 15 per cent in the US and the UK is contrasted with Israel's 25 per cent, (of civilian employment in each case). The gap appears in almost all subdivisions of the sector, with the possible exception of local authorities and business services. The main points of overconcentration (in absolute, but not necessarily in relative terms) are central government, education, health and welfare.

In Israel 7 to 8 per cent of employed persons work in central government and local authorities, [52] a figure considerably higher than in the US and the UK. Employment in the national institutions (about

[51] G.J. Stigler, *op. cit.,* p. 91, Table 31.
[52] These are the services items where there is the greatest relative difference between Census and LFS data. Apart from factors mentioned in our earlier discussion of the problem, there are also classification differences, due mainly to the difficulty of deciding whether a government employee comes under administration (general government) or health or transportation, etc. In this respect also, the LFS data appear to be more consistent with our definition.

0.7 per cent) must be added to the Israel figure, so that the gap is even wider.

Taken separately, the figures suggest that most of the Israel over-concentration is in central rather than local government; however, countries (especially those of Table 2.7) differ considerably in the allo-cation of functions between the two. In the US, local government includes the state administration; and many functions (such as police, welfare, etc.) which in Israel are the province of central government, are locally administered in the UK. Nevertheless it seems plausible that the central government is the focal point of overconcentration in Israel —certainly, if the national institutions are included. [53]

In 'other public services' there is a wide gap in education, health, and welfare and religious services. It is difficult to draw any conclusions about other community services and business services, but here Israel does not appear to deviate so much. [54]

There are no data available which show whether there is any connexion between income level and the employment share of general government, and we must therefore make do with an unsophisticated comparison which ignores this criterion. However, a striking correlation has been found between the employment shares of 'other public ser-vices' and income level. The gap in this sector, especially in education and health, between Israel and the US (and, as far as can be inferred, the UK) is in marked contrast to this finding, and requires explanation.

We have no suitable breakdown of product originating in 'other services' (excluding finance and ownership of dwellings). [55] Neverthe-less, we can state fairly confidently that any overconcentration of product does not stem from the personal services. This conclusion is

[53] In Israel, the item 'National institutions etc.' (see Table 2.7) includes also persons employed in various associations and organizations (such as trade unions, political parties, and similar bodies). In the US data, these are apparently included partly in 'welfare, religious, and other services,' and partly in 'legal and business' services.

[54] The Israel figure (including the relevant part of 'trade and other organi-zations') is 1.5 to 2 per cent. Compared with the US figure of 2.5 per cent (which includes some repair workers) there does not seem to be any con-siderable divergence.

[55] The international statistics of industrial origin of product distinguish 'public administration and defence' and 'other services', but the distinction between administrative and other public sector functions is most inconsistently carried out.

borne out by the employment findings in personal services, and, as will be seen, by the product-worker ratio. [56]

Most of Israel's OS product (as well as employment), originates in general government and in other public institutions (except for ownership of dwellings and personal services). Attempts have been made to find a connexion between economic development and various indicators of government activity (share of product, public consumption and the like); most of the studies have not succeeded in reaching any clearcut conclusion. The principal difficulty encountered is that the institutional structure of public services differs considerably among countries. Of particular interest is the work of Oshima, who found a clear positive connexion between economic development and the ratio of government receipts (excluding deficit) to national income. [57] This study compares about 30 countries, at several periods. The product share of the public sector in general, and of central government in particular, depends, *inter alia,* on the sector's ability to mobilize resources, and not on its economic success in selling its services. If there is a connexion between the public sector's ability to mobilize resources and the income level, we have here a starting point in our search for the cause of the public sector's high product share in Israel. We shall refer to this study in greater detail in the next chapter.

Stigler's data on the product-worker ratio in several 'other services' branches in the US throw some light on this incomplete picture.[58] Comparison with the corresponding Israel data suggests that while in personal, recreation, and (private) professional services the product-worker ratio is higher in Israel than in the US, the converse is true of government services. No reliance should be placed on this rather random comparison, since many explanations could be advanced for the findings. Nevertheless, the figures suggest some degree of employment overconcentration in general government. If there is a negative connexion between product-worker ratio and income level—as has indeed been found—then most of the findings seem normal, except, as stated, in the case of general government.

[56] The product share of recreation was 0.68 per cent in the US (1950) and 0.9 per cent in Israel (1961); of domestic services, 1.11 per cent (US) and 0.6 per cent (Israel), and of 'other personal services', 1.19 per cent (US) and 0.8 per cent (Israel). (From Table 2.1. and G.J. Stigler, *op. cit.,* p. 10, Table 5.)

[57] H. T. Oshima, "Share of Government in Gross National Product for Various Countries," *The American Economic Review,* June 1957, pp. 381–90.

[58] G.J. Stigler, *op. cit.,* p. 10, Table 5.

4. SUMMARY

The following principal conclusions emerge from this chapter.

a.   The income level criterion shows that there is overconcentration of employment in Israel's services. The product-worker ratio does not, however, show any such deviation. This is also reflected by the fact that the product share of services is higher in Israel than in other countries.

b.   The overconcentration of employment is found mainly in general government, education, health, welfare, and religious services. There is some overconcentration in the T+C sector, but it must be stressed that trade is not significantly affected.

c.   The product-worker ratio in the services sub-branches does not diverge from that in countries of the same income level. In particular, no deviations (beyond the margin of error of the data) were found in branches in which there is employment overconcentration. This finding is of great analytical importance, as will be seen in the following chapters, where we apply criteria other than income level.

d.   The predictions of employment share made by the regression method are close to the group averages, when using the country data for both. Considerably different results were obtained when the prediction was made from the regression for the American states. At best, this shows that the behaviour of the employment share of services (and component branches) is bound to be different within the group I income level (nearly all the states fall into this group). If this view is accepted it can be said that at high income levels the tendency for the employment share of services to rise becomes more moderate. This is true also for commerce and the OS sector. In other words, the line which predicts the employment share of services from the income level is not straight, but has a declining slope as income rises.

In the regression for product-worker ratio (calculated from the countries data), the lack of linear fit is more striking. By and large the product-worker ratio declines as income increases, more rapidly at the lower than the higher income levels.

Chapter 3: Causes of Israel's Excess of Services

This chapter seeks to answer the question—and it is the principal question of the study—of what are the economic, social or historical explanations of the gap between the volume of services in Israel and in countries of a similar level of development or per capita income.

Explanatory factors can be classified according to several systems. One way would be to distinguish between those applicable everywhere, and those peculiar to Israel. The first would include diseconomies of scale which can lead to a relative inefficiency of the public services of small countries; or the foreign trade specialization effect, where a comparative advantage in export services might lead to overconcentration of services as a whole.

Examples of the second are Israel's large import surplus, the special needs which govern the country's public demand, supply effects induced by the rapid rate of population growth and the occupational structure of the additional population. This group of factors is the one frequently referred to in the economic literature of Israel. [1]

Another system would list (a) the country's economic ties; (b) demand factors; and (c) supply factors, especially manpower.

In this chapter we use neither of these systems, but shall deal with the various explanations in order of (quantitative) importance. We shall first discuss the effect on industrial structure of Israel's foreign trade, and then move on to specific causes of overconcentration in public services. The main discussion of the supply factor (mass immigration and its occupational structure) is left to the following chapters.

Our discussion rests on theoretical considerations and on information about the country's economy; wherever possible, however, we seek confirmation for our thesis from international comparisons, and from the correlations which have been found between per capita national income and the employment share of various services. In particular, we try to determine to what extent the factors found applicable in Israel explain similar variations in employment shares in other countries.

---

[1] See for example, M. Michaely, *Foreign Trade and Capital Import in Israel*, Am Oved, 1963, pp. 45–48 (Hebrew), and D. Patinkin, *The Israel Economy: The First Decade*, FP, Jerusalem, 1960, pp. 40 ff.

1. THE IMPORT SURPLUS

The import surplus may affect economic growth in two ways, which may be called the income effect and the substitution effect.

The import surplus adds to the economy's national-product-derived resources, and to personal incomes from national income. Since a positive correlation has been found between per capita national income and the employment share of services, it may be asked whether Israel should not be compared with other countries in terms of per capita resources rather than per capita national income.

The basket of goods and services traded in the international market is much more goods-intensive than the home-produced basket. This is because some services cannot enter international trade, while others can do so only at considerable cost. An import surplus which consists for the most part of goods therefore induces the economy to shift from the production of goods to the production of services in order to achieve a balance between goods and services. This is the substitution effect of the import surplus and the specific concomitant of a large import surplus, being distinct from a similar substitution effect which may stem from a country's comparative advantage in the production of services. With the latter, factors of production may shift to services even when there is no surplus or deficit on current balance of payments account. This third possibility may be called the foreign trade specialization effect. [2]

The size of Israel's import surplus, as a percentage of national product or of resources, is unique; there are only a few countries whose import surplus exceeds 2 to 3 per cent of product. For this reason, our regressions need not be recalculated to include import (or export) surplus, and we thus implicitly assume that the specialization effect does not bias the regression even when there is no surplus or deficit on current balance of payments. Nevertheless, for the few countries which have an import surplus it is of interest to discover whether its size and the industrial structure are connected.

---

[2] We shall abbreviate the terms according to the following scheme:

import surplus effect $\left\{\begin{array}{l}\text{income effect} \\ \text{substitution effect} \\ \text{specialization effect}\end{array}\right.$ $\left.\begin{array}{l} \\ \end{array}\right\}$ foreign trade effect

Throughout we are interested only in the broad distinction between goods and services, and in shifts from one to the other.

The income effect

In 1961, Israel's import surplus was $400 million, or about $183 per capita. On this basis, per capita total resources at the disposal of the economy are about $810 (=627+183). The employment share of services as predicted by our regression lines for a level of per capita resources of $810 is shown in Table 3.1.

TABLE 3.1   *The Income Effect of the Import Surplus on the Employment Share of Services*

(per cent)

	Israel 1961[a]	Prediction for per capita income of:		*(1)–(2)*	*(1)–(3)*	*Income effect (4)–(5)*
		$627	*$810*[b]			
	(1)	*(2)*	*(3)*	*(4)*	*(5)*	*(6)*
S	50.0	36.3	40.4	13.7	9.6	4.1
T+C	20.1	17.0	19.5	3.1	0.6	2.5
T	8.2	6.1	7.1	2.1	1.1	1.0
C	11.9	10.9	12.4	1.0	–0.5	1.5
OS	29.9	19.5	21.0	10.4	8.9	1.5

[a] Labour Force Survey figures.
[b] Based on import surplus of $400 million, or $183 per capita. The prediction was calculated as explained in Table 2.6 for $627.
SOURCE: Columns (1) and (2) from Table 2.6, panel B. Column (3) calculated from the Kuznets *Countries* data in the same way as column (2).

Taking the figures at their face value, we find that the income effect is considerable: it explains about 4 percentage points of the services employment share. This is from one quarter to one third of the gap between Israel's level and the norm.[3] But this is not enough. We must take into account several factors which may either intensify or weaken the income effect, and which are all connected with the difference between a domestic and a foreign income increment.

Let us assume a hypothetical case: an external addition to the economy's income is allocated to the various economic units in the same proportions as would occur with additional future income produced by the economy itself. Let us further assume that the recipients of the

---

[3] Within services, all the excess in commerce, and half the excess in transportation are explained, while 'other services' are little affected by the income effect.

additional external income behave as though it were ordinary income from ordinary sources. A third assumption is required to isolate the substitution effect: that the foreign purchases acquired with the additional income have the same branch-of-origin composition as the economy's own production. In this case it can be said, on purely theoretical grounds, that the effect on the composition of final demand will be identical with the effect of an increase in income derived from internal sources; hence, the effect of final demand on industrial structure will also be the same. However, even under our assumptions, industrial structure will not be affected from the supply and production side. The additional income was not derived from within the economy; therefore it does not induce changes in production methods and relative productivity levels of various branches or in the important intermediate component of demand. [4]

Some of the structural change accompanying economic development may be due to autonomous [5] developments on the supply side, but no such changes can be expected to result from an increase in external income. If we assume that demand and supply effects both operate in the same direction, we can expect an externally derived increase in income to have a smaller effect on the employment share of services than an increase in income derived from national product. In fact, as we saw in the preceding chapter, various investigators explain an increase in the employment share of services partly in terms of changes in relative productivity and in nominal product per worker. Both Kuznets and Clark, who stress the importance of the increase in demand for services, also stress the importance of business services.

If we drop the first two of our assumptions, the demand effect of additional resources derived from an import surplus will still not be the same as for an 'internal' increment. In fact, the assumptions are not valid, at any rate for Israel. The allocation of the external increment undoubtedly differs from the expected allocation of a product increment. We shall not discuss all the possible results of such differences—indeed, this can only be done *ex post*. We shall confine ourselves to noting an important distinction, observable in Israel, between the two types of

[4]   a. The addition to the economy's productive capacity due to the import surplus of previous years is already taken into account in the national product of a given year.

     b. On producers' demand for services see, for example, C. Clark, *The Conditions of Economic Progress* (third edition), London 1957, p. 376.

[5]   'Autonomous' must be stressed, since changes in demand conditions will induce some supply changes.

resource increment. The public sector receives the bulk of Israel's additional external resources and decides how they are to ~~~~ed [6] It is unlikely that the public sector would receive the same ~~~tion of a product increment. This difference in allocation is likely to affect the development of services in two different ways: first, and perhaps more important, an external increment will raise the employment, and hence the product share of 'other services' more than will an internal increment. Clearly, this is due to the increased share of public services. Second, the allocation of the increment (to public or private recipients) means that the share of several privately supplied services—in particular, trade—will increase less if the increment is external. The additional income used directly by the public sector is not likely to increase the employment share of trade (and personal services) as much as a resource increment allocated to all economic units.

As explained in Chapter 2, we cannot accurately predict the effect on the product-worker ratio of an addition to resources or income, especially when the changes in income or resource level are very slight. Nevertheless, the theory may be advanced that a resource increment derived from the import surplus will not in any way affect the ratio. This follows from our discussion in Chapter 2; the decline in the product-worker ratio of services as the economy develops was there explained mainly in terms of factors operating from the supply side and the production system: we here argue that the import surplus has little effect on the production system.

The substitution effect

That foreign trade affects economic structure is well-known and requires no proof. Kuznets at the outset excludes from the relevant country-groups small countries whose foreign economic ties are likely to create a structure unlike that found in larger, economically independent countries; this is not, however, to ignore the fact that foreign links have some effect in all countries. [7] When comparing the supply of services in various countries and correlating it with the income level, Clark introduces an international trade correction in order to determine the composition of resource use instead of the composition of own production, which may be adapted to international exchange. [8] It can

---

[6] According to Michaely's calculations, the public sector received 75 per cent of the capital transfers during 1949–59, individuals receiving only 25 per cent. See M. Michaely, *op. cit.,* p. 36.

[7] S. Kuznets, *Countries,* p. 6.

[8] C. Clark, *op. cit.,* p. 378.

be argued that structural shifts between goods and services (when imports balance exports) do not occur as frequently as specialization in certain goods. However, if we consider transportation, tourist services, and several other business services, we see that such shifts are not, after all, so rare. [9] Nevertheless, the international trade basket undoubtedly contains a greater proportion of goods than the various countries' production baskets. It follows that the industrial structure of countries with an import surplus will be more strongly affected than that of countries whose imports and exports balance. Our question is: what would Israel's industrial structure be in the absence of the import surplus? In substitution effect terms, what would the structure be if the economy did not have to produce a high proportion of services in order to supplement the goods-intensive import basket? The answer may be found by examining the branch composition of total resources rather than of product, in respect of both value added and employment. We shall do this by combining the industrial structure of product and import surplus, using appropriate weights.

Let us briefly define the industrial structure of the import surplus. The import surplus does not have a branch structure in the simple meaning of the term, and at least two definitions are thus possible:

a. The industrial composition of the import surplus is identical with that of imports, since the import surplus is a residual which cannot be allocated to specific commodities in the import basket.

b. The industrial composition of the import surplus is that of the basket obtained by deducting specific exports from the corresponding imports.

Each of these definitions is appropriate to different questions about the effect of foreign trade on industrial structure, and neither of them provides a precise answer to our question on the substitution effect except in the special case where there is no goods-services specialization in the economy, i.e., when the composition of imports and exports is identical. In this case, both definitions will yield identical results, and only the import surplus effect will be taken into account. In the general case, in which there is some specialization—whether in goods or services

[9] The balance of payments of the UK and the Netherlands provide well-known instances of considerable transportation exports. A more interesting example is the Lebanon which pays for a good part of its merchandise imports by supplying a varied basket of services to the rest of the world. The income from tourism of Switzerland, Italy, France, and other countries, and the financial and insurance services of international financial centres should also be mentioned.

—concept (b) will include both the substitution effect and the full effect of specialization; concept (a) will include some of the specialization effect—that reflected in imports—as well as the substitution effect. A hypothetical model will illustrate these distinctions:

	Total	Goods	Services
		(percent of total)	
1. Product	10	60	40
No specialization			
2. Imports	4	90	10
3. Exports	2	90	10
4. Import surplus (both concepts)	2	90	10
5. Resources (lines 1 and 4)	12	65	35
Specialization in services			
6. Imports	4	95	5
7. Exports	2	70	30
8. Import surplus — concept (a)	2	95	5
9. — concept (b)	2	120	−20
10. Resources — (a) (lines 1 and 8)	12	66	34
11. — (b) (lines 1 and 9)	12	70	30

Line 5 shows only the substitution effect. More precisely, a product structure of 60 goods and 40 services is the result of adaptation to a goods-intensive import surplus; without the surplus, product (if we like, at a product level of 12), would have consisted of 65 goods and 35 services.

A country specializing in services presumably purchases less services from abroad than one which is neutral in this respect. This is reflected in line 6. Specialization is also reflected in exports (compare lines 3 and 7). We have two concepts (lines 8 and 9) of the composition of the import surplus, and will thus get two results for the composition of resources. Line 10 differs somewhat from line 5, since line 10 reflects part of the specialization effect (the part due to the difference in the import composition). Line 11 in turn differs from line 10, since here the rest of the specialization effect has been taken into account. We can assume that the resource structure of 70 goods and 30 services is close to the product structure that would prevail in the absence of the economy's import surplus and its foreign trade. [10]

[10] This analysis makes the simplifying assumption that relative-price and other changes are nonexistent or negligible.

TABLE 3.2   *The Composition of the Import Surplus in Israel: 1961*

| | Exports[a] | Imports[a] | Import surplus[b] | Composition of exports (per cent) | Composition of import surplus[c] (per cent) | | | |
| | | | | | Unadjusted[a] | | Adjusted[c] | |
	(1)	(2)	(3)	(4)	Concept (a) (5)	Concept (b) (6)	Concept (a) (7)	Concept (b) (8)
	(millions of dollars)							
Total	**384.8**	**732.5**	**347.7**	**100.0**	100.0	100.0	100	100
Total merchandise	252.4	586.1	333.7	65.6	80.0	96.0	75	81
Merchandise[f]	244.9	525.6	280.7	63.6	71.7	80.7		
Government n.e.s.	7.5	60.5	53.0	2.0	8.3	15.3		
Services	132.4	146.4	14.0	34.4	20.0	4.0	25	19
Transportation	65.5	81.1	15.6	17.0	11.1	4.5		
Insurance	26.0	31.8	5.8	6.8	4.3	1.7		
Trade, business and other services	10.6	15.2	4.6	2.7	2.1	1.3		
Foreign travel	30.3	18.3	-12.0	7.9	2.5	-3.5		

[a] The source figures have been reclassified as follows:
1. Imports and exports of capital services are excluded, since there is no way of classifying them by industrial origin. The implied assumption is that the breakdown is proportional to that of other items.

2. Construction activities and sales and purchases of ships' fuel included in the source item 'other services' have been shifted to merchandise.

3. Communications transactions have been shifted from 'other services' to transportation.

4. The item government n.e.s. is here classified as merchandise.
Nevertheless, the division into goods and services here shown is still not fully accurate:
   (i) Although most of the item government n.e.s. is connected with Ministry of Defence expenditures, the rest is in fact services (Foreign Ministry outlays, and Bond Drive costs).
   (ii) Transportation and tourism (most of 'foreign travel') include some goods transactions.
   (iii) Insurance services consist of premiums and claims paid. Only about 20 per cent of the amounts shown are relevant for our purpose.
In all, services are thus somewhat overstated, in particular because of the third factor (iii).

b The following points should be borne in mind as regards the merchandise-services composition of the import surplus [see also note a, (i) to (iii)]:
   1. Net services import in government n.e.s. does not exceed 2 per cent of import surplus.
   2. Net foreign travel exports include some merchandise; this results in an understatement of not more than 1 per cent (of import surplus) in net import of services. (Net imports of transportation also include some merchandise.)
   3. If we assume that net insurance imports are mostly the profits of foreign insurance companies, this item is not biased.
In all, the net import of services may be understated, but by no more than 1 to 2 per cent (of import surplus).

c Concept (a)—Calculated from column (2), imports.
d Concept (b)—Calculated from column (3), import surplus. See pp. 44-45 in the text.
e Except as explained in note a.
e Adjustment was made in order to arrive at the value-added distribution of the import surplus (in addition to adjustments for the net bias described in notes a and b). This is based on an estimate (at ex factory cost) of net goods input in final services and of the services input of final goods output, according to Bruno (see Source).
The adjustments to columns (5) and (6) are as follows:

	Concept (a)	Concept (b)
	(per cent of import surplus)	
1. Value added adjustment	+8	+13
2. Other adjustments (see notes a and b)	−3 to 4	+1 to 2
Total	+5	+15

   (+) is a shift to services; (−) is a shift to goods.
f Includes non-monetary gold.

SOURCE: CBS, *SAI 1963*, No. 14, p. 408, Table 2 (Balance of Payments).
Input coefficients from M. Bruno, *Interdependence, Resource Use, and Structural Change in Israel*, Bank of Israel Research Department, Special Studies No. 2, Jerusalem 1962, p. 25, Table I-6.

We have so far ignored a third factor which may affect the composition of imports [or of import surplus (a)] and which is of particular
importance in Israel. This is the import component of exports. The
export of services (whether specialized or not) may require an imported
services input. To illustrate: transport services are a major item in
Israel's services exports, while the payments by Israeli overseas transport
companies for the services of foreign ports and airports are an important
element of transport imports. If this import component is of sufficient
weight, it can offset the specialization effect illustrated earlier. For
example, import surplus (a) might, under these conditions, consist of
85 goods and 15 services (see line 8 of the example). In this case the
concept (a) resources structure might reflect less than the total import
surplus substitution effect.

In general, the specialization effect is in the same direction as the
substitution effect in an economy specializing in services; if the economy
specializes in goods the effects act in opposing directions.

TABLE 3.3   *The Foreign Trade Effects*[a] *on Industrial Structure*

(*per cent*)

	Explanation in terms of		The share of services		Based on column in Table 3.2
	Product share	Employment share	Resources[d]	Import Surplus	
	57.1 less (4)[b]	(1) × 0.9[c]			
	(1)	(2)	(3)	(4)	
1. *The substitution effect of import surplus* [concept (a)]					
a. Unadjusted	8.4	7.6	48.7	20	(5)
b. Adjusted[e]	7.3	6.6	49.8	25	(7)
2. *The foreign trade effect* [concept (b)]					
a. Unadjusted	12.0	10.8	45.1	4	(6)
b. Adjusted[e]	8.6	7.7	48.5	19	(8)

[a] See text, pp. 40 ff; and note 2 on p. 40.
[b] 57.1 is the share of services in product (Table 2.6).
[c] The product-worker ratio of services is about 1.1; the employment share
therefore declines by 0.9 percentage points for every percentage point decline
in product share.
[d] Calculated from product and import surplus shares with weights of 77.4 and
22.6 per cent, respectively. (Based on national income of IL 4,119 million,
or $ 1,373 million at IL 3/$ 1, and import surplus of $ 400 million).
[e] Including value added adjustment.
SOURCE: Tables 3.2 and 2.6.

The conventional classification of foreign trade statistics does not reflect the relevant structure of the import surplus. In the case of product, we are interested in the value added by industrial origin; for imports, the relevant breakdown is also in terms of value added. An industrial good as defined in the import statistics is a combination of the added values of several branches; an imported service is likewise composed of inputs from other branches. The composition of imports relevant for our purpose is thus not that of the goods and services entering the country, but the value added composition of the producing branches. Lack of information and other technical difficulties prevent us from breaking imports down in this manner, but the problem cannot be ignored.

Table 3.2 adapts Israel's foreign trade data for combination with the branch structure of product. Columns (5) and (6) show the breakdown for concepts (a) and (b) respectively.[11] Columns (7) and (8) show an attempt to approach a classification of added values instead of final output; this was the largest adjustment made (see notes to table). The adjustments are rather crude, and should be treated with caution; nevertheless, it seems to us, for reasons which will not be discussed here, that the estimates of the share of services in the import surplus as shown in columns (7) and (8) at the least provide an upper limit and that for our purposes these figures are preferable to these shown in columns (5) and (6). Table 3.3 summarizes the effect of these calculations on the substitution and specialization effects, according to each of columns (5) to (8) of Table 3.2.

The results of the exercise can be summarized in two parts: the effect on the share of services as a whole, and the effect on the shares of several sub-groups.

The share of all services in resources according to import surplus (a) is 48.5 to 50 per cent (lines 1.a and 1.b of Table 3.3). This is to say that the crude substitution effect raises the product share of services by at least 7 per cent of total product or 12 per cent of product originating in services. The share of services in resources according to import surplus (b) comes to 45 to 48.5 per cent, and the foreign trade effect comes to at least 8 or 9 per cent of product, or 20 per cent of product originating in services (lines 2.a and 2.b).

As stated, there is no precise way of separating the substitution and specialization effects. If it is assumed that the (positive or negative)

---

[11] Some adjustments, explained in note a to Table 3.2, have been made to the official statistics.

specialization effect added to the concept (a) import surplus effect is small, more than four fifths of the total effect may be ascribed to substitution, and only about one fifth to specialization. These effects, even when the lower limit is taken, explain a considerable part of the over-concentration in services.

Column 2 of Table 3.3 shows a, perhaps rash, attempt to estimate these effects also in terms of employment shares. The estimate is based on the finding that the product-worker ratio in services (see Table 2.6) is about 1.10, so that a one per cent decline in the product share reduces the employment share by 0.9 per cent.[12] The results show that the employment share of services is raised by 6.5 to 7.5 percentage points by the substitution effect alone, and by the total foreign trade effect in the range of 7.5 to 11 percentage points: i.e., the import surplus in particular, and foreign trade in general, has a marked effect on the overconcentration of economic activity in the services. In relative terms, more than half the gap between the employment share in Israel and the normal level (as defined in the previous chapter), can be explained in this way.

We have seen that foreign trade is more goods intensive than is product. However, not all services are under-represented in import surplus to the same extent; the data show that the import surplus contains much transportation and commerce and very little 'other,' particularly public, services.

On the one hand, the substitution effect tends to be concentrated in 'other services': the 7 percentage points explained by the substitution effect are a much higher proportion of the 10-point excess in this sector than of the excess in all services together. [13] Moreover, since the product-worker ratio of 'other services' is less than unity, a 1 per cent change in the product share will generate a change in employment of more than 1 per cent. On the other hand, the picture is consistent with the finding that there is no serious overconcentration in transportation and commerce. [14]

---

12 The average product-worker ratio for all services has been used on the first assumption that the foreign trade effects are spread equally over the services sub-groups. We drop this assumption later.

13 The specialization effect is not important in these branches: as can be seen in Table 3.2, it is transportation and tourism which show the biggest difference between concept (a) and concept (b).

14 Patinkin writes in this connexion: "But [the substitution effect] can be only part of the explanation—for otherwise we should expect to find the percentage of the labor force in commerce and transportation to be 'abnormal' to

The data appear to confirm our hypothesis, even though it is not possible to carry out precise computations.

First, foreign trade or at least the import surplus seems, from the available data, to have very little effect on the size of the transportation branch and perhaps even reduces its share in Israel. The share of transportation is evidently greater in import surplus (a) [column (5) of Table 3.2] than in product. Even in import surplus (b) [column (6)], the share of transport seems to be no lower than in product, since some of the services value added which is 'hidden' in the value of goods, probably originates in transportation. [15]

Second, a smaller share of the import surplus as shown in columns (5) and (6) of Table 3.2 originates in wholesale trade, finance and insurance. On the other hand, it may be assumed that these constitute a considerable proportion of the services input of goods. In other words, a good part of the 15 per cent (net) transferred from goods to services in column (8) belongs to these branches. Naturally, retail trade is not represented in foreign trade.

Theoretical considerations, supported by the 1961 foreign trade data, lead to the following conclusions about the import surplus effect (and the total foreign trade effect) on the industrial structure of Israel. Both the income effect and the substitution effect—but principally the latter—explain most of the overconcentration of economic activity in services. A further explanation is provided by the foreign trade specialization effect. Both the income and the substitution effect of the import surplus

---

roughly the same extent as in [other] services. The fact that this is not so indicates that other factors are also at work here ..." (*op. cit.*, p. 42). Our findings show that it is not for this reason that the explanation is incomplete.

[15] The share of transportation in product is 7.5 per cent. This is compared with 11.1 per cent [column (5) of Table 3.2] which also includes purchases of goods, and with 4.5 per cent in column (6); to the latter must be added 5 per cent of the value of goods shown in the column—approximately the rate of transportation input of the goods at ex factory cost. (See M. Bruno, *Interdependence, Resource Use, and Structural Change in Israel*, Bank of Israel Research Department, Special Studies 2, 1962, Table M–5 (in folder). The impression given by the transport data in columns (5) and (6) or (7) as compared with column (8) is that while the substitution effect (in addition to the effect of the import component of transportation exports) tends to raise the share of transport in the economy, exports explain a considerable part of the increase; it may be said that the substitution effect offsets the specialization effect.

TABLE 3.4   *The Employment Share of Services in Various Countries:*
Deviations of Actual Shares from the
Regression Prediction

(*percentage points*)

	S	T	C	OS
A. Positive deviations[a][b]				
Israel[c]	13.7–16.2	2.1–2.4	1.0–1.4	10.4–12.2
Argentina	14.2	1.3	3.8	9.0
Netherlands	14.0	1.9	4.4	7.7
Ceylon	12.2	0.4	1.2	10.0
Chile	11.3	0.8	1.6	8.5
Jamaica	10.1	.. [d]	0.5	12.8
Cuba	8.8	1.6	3.5	3.3
Puerto Rico	8.2	0.7	1.7	5.4
United Kingdom	7.8	2.4	1.8	3.4
Panama	6.9	..	..	..
Venezuela	6.2	−2.2	−1.4	9.7
Australia	5.7	1.0	1.5	3.1
Ireland	5.4	0.6	2.0	2.5
B. Negative deviations[a][b]				
Turkey	19.9	3.0	6.8	10.9
Honduras	16.0	2.2	5.7	8.6
Belgian Congo	15.1	1.9	5.1	8.7
United States	11.1	4.8	2.7	3.3
Thailand	11.0	2.2	+1.5	10.3
Finland	10.4	0.4	3.2	6.9
Guatemala	8.6	1.8	1.5	5.9
Switzerland	8.0	3.7	2.4	1.9
Pakistan	7.5	1.4	1.2	5.3
Peru	6.3	1.3	2.2	3.4

[a] Actual *less* prediction. A plus sign in panel B indicates a positive deviation.
[b] The standard deviation of the predictions increases with the distance of the country's per capita income from the all-country average.
[c] The range is that given by the two estimates, the first figure being from the LFS data.
[d] Included in OS.
SOURCE: Israel—Table 2.6, panel B.
　　　　　Other countries—Regression calculated from the country data in S. Kuznets, *Countries.*

act mainly on 'other services' and within these mainly on public services. [16]

International comparison

Does the experience of other countries support our conclusions in any way? As a starting point for answering this and other questions we constructed a table showing the more extreme deviations of employment shares from the regression lines for total services and for important service sub-sectors (Table 3.4). There are six countries (including Israel) in which the employment share of services exceeds the predicted share by 10 per cent or more, and seven countries in which the deviation is 5 to 9 per cent.

What we now want to test is whether countries with a permanent heavy deficit on current balance of payments are those which show services overconcentration. [17]

Of the six countries with an import surplus of more than 5 per cent of national product in the early 1950's and for which we had employment data, five (including Israel) showed overconcentration in services. The other four are Puerto Rico, Venezuela, Ireland, and Panama, and in each the employment share of services deviates from the norm by 5 to 8 per cent. The country with an import surplus but without services overconcentration is Greece. Import surpluses of less than 5 per cent of product were not found to be associated with services overconcentration. [18] In Israel, Venezuela, and Puerto Rico (and apparently also in Panama), the principal overconcentration is in the OS sector.

2. RESOURCES AT THE DISPOSAL OF THE PUBLIC SECTOR

In Chapter 2 we saw that the principal point of overconcentration in Israel is services supplied by the public sector (general government and private nonprofit institutions). [19] In the preceding section we saw

---

[16] It should perhaps be said that the income and substitution effects, as here calculated, do not overlap, but are additive.

[17] There is no reason for the converse to hold: overconcentration in services can have many other causes.

[18] Figures on balance of payments deficit: D. Patinkin, *op. cit.*, p. 51, Figure 3, and M. Michaely, *op. cit.*, p. 40, Table 19. We could find no employment data for South Korea and Southern Rhodesia which also have a high import surplus.

[19] There is no information on employment by type of institution, although there is a breakdown for product: in 1961, IL 110 million of product of

that a considerable part of the excess can be explained in terms of the
different foreign trade effects, but this is not the whole picture. In
this and the following three sections we explore also the possible effects
of the supply and demand conditions prevailing in the public sector
in Israel.

When applied to public sector services, the terms supply and demand
do not mean the same as when applied to ordinary markets. When we
speak of demand for public sector services we mean the whole economy's
demand function, which is mainly expressed in the decisions of the
governing institutions: the demand of individuals is expressed through
the representative and political framework. In everyday (and imprecise)
terms, one speaks of the country's public services requirements. By the
supply conditions of public sector services we mean primarily the problem
of mobilizing the economic resources which enable the government and
other public bodies to supply services. This problem stems from the
fact that public services are for the most part not sold and indeed are
often not received by individuals (e.g., defence, administration, public
health). The necessary resources are usually mobilized by imposing taxes
on the population, and most of these are not, from the taxpayer's point
of view, connected with the services supplied. A second supply problem
is the complex one of the productivity of public sector activities.

In the following sections we attempt to show that for several services
requirements are greater in Israel than in the other countries compared.
Owing to the difficulty of distinguishing between requirements and
lack of efficiency, we shall combine our discussion of the two. In this
section we deal with the possible effect of supply conditions, i.e., the
possibility of mobilizing resources in Israel as compared with other
countries.

There is overconcentration of product and employment in the public
services, while the product-worker ratio is not remarkably low; this itself
is evidence that the public sector has at its disposal the economic
resources required to supply services at a higher rate (as a share of
product) than other countries. Something has already been said about
additional resources in the earlier discussion on the destination of the
import surplus (p. 42), and we shall return to this subject in greater
detail.

---

public services originated in private profit-making enterprise. This is about
2.5 per cent of total product, and about 12 per cent of the public services
product, and covers most of the item business and legal services and about
20 per cent of health services (according to NAD data).

The argument underlying the present discussion may be stated as follows: first, a public sector as a rule wishes to supply more services than it has means for. In other words, the effective restraint on the volume of public sector services is one of resources rather than demand. The term 'resource restraint' is here not intended to refer to the first law of economics—the law of scarcity—but to the more prosaic economic, political, and social fact that there is an upper limit to the amount that a government can reasonably mobilize from internal sources. Second, and more important, Israel and a few other countries have been able to raise this ceiling well above what is usually attainable. Such additional resources were used to supply public sector services, at a higher level than in countries restricted to their tax potential—regardless of special needs, or of whether the additional resources are devoted to important and essential purposes or 'wasted' on unessentials.

The first part of our statement relies on two studies which showed clearly a positive connexion betwen level of development and total government revenue (excluding deficit) or per capita public expenditure.[20] The hypothesis which Oshima attempts to test in his study is a variant of the tax capacity theory which states that the ability of the government to impose taxes is a function chiefly of the economy's level of development. [21] It is not our purpose here to discuss the validity of the tax capacity theory, and our statement still stands if we modify the expression 'tax capacity' (which sets a maximum budget) to an 'optimum budget', which equates the marginal social welfare of the additional services with the marginal social damage of the additional taxes; all this holds not only from an economic, but also from a political viewpoint. Oshima, Fabricant and others have shown that the limit depends principally on the economy's level of development, and specifically on the level of per capita national income, but also on a long list of other factors—among them the regime's ideological colour and its stability, and the structure and organization of the economy.

[20] H. T. Oshima "Share of Government in Gross National Product for Various Countries," *The American Economic Review*, XLVII, June 1957, 381–90 and S. Fabricant, *Trends in Government Activity Since 1900*, NBER, New York, 1952, Chapter 6.

The first (government revenue and level of development) deals with 31 countries. Fabricant (per capita public expenditure) deals with state and local administration in the American states; he found that urbanization and population density had little effect on the per capita level of public outlays.

[21] Fabricant, on the other hand, speaks more in terms of "ability to pay, or needs" than in terms of optimum budget. *Ibid.*, pp. 121–22.

However, since the level of development provides the chief explanation of the behaviour of government revenues, we may conclude (as does Oshima, and, to some extent, Fabricant) that most governments in the world wish to supply their populations with a greater volume of services than permitted by their powers of taxation in the prevailing economic and political constellation. Political and economic limitations are thus the effective checks on the activities of the public sector; as soon as additional resources are available [22] governments will seize the opportunity to expand their services.

Oshima illustrates his findings by dividing his 31 countries into two groups: undeveloped countries in which he found that government receipts are between 8 and 19 per cent of GNP, and developed countries in which the corresponding figures are between 20 and 35 per cent. To this general positive connexion we have added a statistical test which shows a very high correlation between per capita income (from Kuznets' data) and government revenue (from Oshima) : [23] the correlation coefficient (for Oshima's countries) was 0.64. Deviations from the regression line are however of greater interest. Oshima discusses the low government revenue figure found for the United States, and explains the deviation in terms of the private enterprise ideology which predominates in this country. Other countries for which the ideological explanation perhaps holds are Canada and Switzerland (downwards deviations) and the UK (upward deviation).

Another type of deviation from the norm is due to a resource effect: there may be more, or politically and economically cheaper, resources than are usually available. Cited by Oshima as a typical example of this is Ceylon, which has the fourth lowest per capita income of the countries shown; taxes in this country come to 19 per cent of GNP because it is easier to tax the tea exports which are the country's principal source of wealth than to levy income and other internal taxes. Oshima also mentions in this connexion the taxation imposed by Venezuela on the oil companies. It is difficult to generalize conclusions

[22] On any terms, according to the 'tax capacity' approach, or more cheaply, according to the 'optimum budget' concept.

[23] The regressions from Oshima's data are:

I. For 31 countries: $GR = 12 \cdot 10^{-3} x + 15.0,$ $r = 0.64$
$$(27 \cdot 10^{-4})$$

II. Excluding Canada and the United States:
$$GR = 19 \cdot 10^{-3} x + 12.0,$$ $r = 0.75$
$$(33 \cdot 10^{-4})$$

where GR is government revenue and x is per capita income.

CAUSES OF ISRAEL'S EXCESS OF SERVICES   57

without a close examination of each country, but the statement about
Ceylon and Venezuela is borne out by our findings on the deviation in
services employment. Both in Ceylon and Venezuela there is overconcentration in services, in both cases mostly in the OS sector (Table
3.4).

Israel is undoubtedly a striking example of a deviation from the
norm due to the fact that the public sector has considerable nontax
resources at its disposal. So far account has been taken—in particular
in Oshima's study—only of taxes and other revenues that are not

TABLE 3.5   *Public Sector*[a] *Receipts in Israel: 1961*

	Total in IL million	Per cent of total			
		Foreign sources[b c]	Domestic sources		
			Total	Taxes	Other[b] receipts
A. General government	2,349[d]	22.1	77.9	61.3	16.6
Central government	1,908	19.8	80.2	68.5	11.7
Local authorities	292	1.7	98.3	45.6	52.7
National institutions	216	62.7	37.3	–	37.3
B. Private nonprofit institutions[e]	450	19.5	80.5	–	80.5
C. Total public sector	2,724[f]	22.3	77.7	52.8	24.9
D. C as per cent of resources[g]	44.3	9.9	34.4	23.4	11.0

[a] The definition does not correspond to that of 'public services' as used in
Chapter 2 and elsewhere, but includes only general government and nonprofit
institutions serving households. Trade organizations etc. are included in the
latter.
[b] Transfers, loans, short-term credit, etc. Direct sales of goods and services are
a negligible element of 'other receipts.'
[c] At the official exchange rate (IL1.80/$1). See also note 24 on p. 58.
[d] Excludes inter-agency transfers received by local authorities (IL 52 million)
and national institutions (IL 15 million) from the central government.
[e] Excludes transactions between nonprofit institutions.
[f] Excludes IL 75 million received by nonprofit institutions from private sector.
[g] GNP *plus* import surplus.
SOURCE: Bank of Israel, *Annual Report 1961*, as follows:
      Public sector—p. 86, Table VII—3 for percentages, and absolute figures
        from Tables VII–1, VII–6, VII–15 and VII–17.
      Nonprofit institutions—pp. 330–31, Table XVI–1.
      Resources from CBS, *Israel's National Income and Expenditure (1950–
        1962)*, Special Series No. 153, Jerusalem 1964, p. 5, Table 1.

budget deficit; we shall now extend the discussion on Israel to all resources available to the public sector, on the assumption that extra sources are not available to the public sectors of many other countries, at least to the same extent. Table 3.5 shows the composition of Israel's public sector receipts in 1961, and their share in resources. The outstanding features of the table are:

a. Total public sector receipts come to about 45 per cent of resources when nonprofit institutions are included, and to about 38 per cent when they are not.

b. Tax revenues are only about half of total (60 per cent if nonprofit institutions are excluded), so that the tax burden comes to 23 per cent of resources. This seems somewhat high compared with the Oshima results (for an exact comparison some nontax ordinary revenue should be included, which would raise the rate slightly, but not much) [24]

c. About 22 per cent of public sector revenue is derived from foreign sources, which provide 63 per cent of the income of the national institutions, but are also of importance in the income of government and the nonprofit institutions.[25] It should be noted that a sizable part of nontax revenue from internal sources consists of interest and principal receipts on account of loans granted by the government out of its foreign resources.

d. About one quarter (one sixth if nonprofit institutions are excluded) of the receipts derive from domestic nontax sources. These include, in particular, the transfers of households to nonprofit institutions, of which the largest item is dues paid to the Histadrut, in which a considerable part of the population is organized.

All this sufficiently demonstrates the importance of foreign resources in public sector finance. Clearly, also, they cannot be replaced by taxation.

It is perhaps desirable to dwell on the high share of nontax domestic revenues in the total, and especially on the amount (about IL 190 million) of transfers by households to the nonprofit institutions; the latter are today engaged in a wide range of activity; this has come about largely because the most important of them were established

---

[24] It should be remembered that in 1961 some of this taxation was a devaluation substitute. If the devaluation element is netted out, the rate of taxation is lower.

[25] The share of foreign income in the revenue of national and nonprofit institutions is understated in the table, since the domestic revenues include intersectoral transfers (i.e. from the central government). These are, however, excluded from lines A and C (see notes d and f to Table 3.5).

before the State in order to supplement the meagre services provided by the mandatory government. When the State was established, these institutions expanded their activities, while keeping open the financing channels they had developed earlier. In this way internal (and foreign) sources of income were kept, outside the system of taxation, and a large volume of public services was maintained; it is doubtful whether this could have been achieved entirely through taxation.

The discussion so far may have given the misleading impression that all the public sector's revenues are (or were) used to provide services (in the sense in which the word is used in this study). Clearly, a considerable part of public sector outlays are devoted to other fields— direct or indirect investment, transfer payments to households, and debt servicing. We do indeed maintain that the relatively large volume of resources available to Israel's public sector permits, among other things, a greater supply of services than in other countries.

The resource effect, however, goes beyond this. A considerable administrative machine is required in order to mobilize and administer the large volume of resources. We have pointed out that the extra resources available to the public sector are cheaper than taxes and easier to obtain. But by cheaper we refer primarily to social and political difficulties which become more intense the more one attempts to raise taxes. While the extra resources of Israel's public sector are in large measure free from this kind of difficulty, they are costly in manpower and money. One reflection of the price paid for the extra resources is the proliferation of government agencies—apparently a prerequisite for the mobilization of additional resources.

In addition, there may be a willingness to engage in border-line activities of doubtful value in terms of equating marginal cost and marginal social benefit; the subject is explored further in Section 5.

The theory, confirmed by the empirical findings, states that there is an upper limit to the ability of governments to mobilize funds for public purposes, and that this upper limit is closely connected with the country's level of development; thus, the fact that in Israel the ceiling is not effective at the normal level may explain some of the overconcentration in services. The additional resources available to Israel's public sector stem partly from foreign sources, but also from the inherited pre-State machinery of making payments to public bodies that today's public sector has become accustomed to.

3. THE EDUCATION BURDEN

In Chapter 2 we saw that a great deal of public sector overconcentration is in educational services. At the same time no one in any way acquainted with education in this country needs much convincing that there is a serious shortage of educational staff. The use made of untrained conscripts for teaching purposes, and the calls made on former teachers to return to the profession illustrate the shortage. How can the two be reconciled?

Our answer to this question is that Israel combines the demographic characteristics of an undeveloped country with the educational standards of a developed one. This combination imposes an education burden on the country's adult population which is among the highest, if not the highest, in the world.

The employment share of education is a function of three factors:

a.   The proportion of population of school-age.

b.   The proportion of school-age population actually at school.

c.   The number of pupils per person employed in education.

The employment share of education rises as the first two indicators rise, and as the third declines. The age-distribution is entirely a demographic factor; the rate of school-attendance reflects the educational standards that the community sets itself. The pupil-teacher ratio reflects both the intensity and standard of education, and the efficiency of the educational process—elements which it is difficult to distinguish. A low pupil-teacher ratio can reflect, for example, small classes, which can be due to faulty organization, or to a scattered population, or to the desire to give more intensive education. Furthermore, the demographic factor affects not only the number of potential pupils, but also the labour force participation of the whole population. A high proportion of children in the population raises the number of potential pupils while reducing the population from which the educators are drawn: the employment share of education rises on both counts.

Table 3.6 shows indicators representing the three factors mentioned, summarized as averages of the income-level groups. The conclusions that emerge from the table are: [26]

a.   The share of the 5 to 19 age-group in population is highest in the underdeveloped countries (about 33 to 37 per cent); it drops to a low level of 20 to 25 per cent in Western Europe, and is slightly higher

[26] Data for each country included are shown in Appendix C.

TABLE 3.6 *The Education-Burden in Selected Countries: Income-Group Averages*[a]

Income group[b]	Number of countries in group	Per cent of population aged 5–19	Per cent of 5–19 age-group attending school[c]	Pupils per teacher in primary schools	Per cent of population	
					Attending schools[c] $(1) \times (2)$	Teachers[d] $(4) \div (3)$
		(1)	(2)	(3)	(4)	(5)
I	9	23.8	72.1	27.6	17.4	0.63
II	6	26.5	69.8	31.3	18.0	0.59
III	5	30.0	64.6	37.2	19.5	0.56
IV	8	32.8	45.0	35.2	14.5	0.43
V	5	33.2	48.8	46.2	16.1	0.38
VI	6	36.5	39.2	35.2	14.2	0.41
VII	7	33.9	31.6	39.1	10.8	0.28
Israel		32	69	24 [e]	22.1	0.92

[a] Unweighted arithmetic means.
[b] By per capita national product. The grouping is that of the Kuznets study, used elsewhere in the present work.
[c] Primary and secondary schools.
[d] We have implicitly assumed that the pupil-teacher ratio for all forms of education is the same as in primary schools [since column (3) figures refer to primary education only].
[e] The Israel figures are from the international sources. *SAI 1961*, No. 12, gives a pupil-teacher ratio of 26 according to the number of teachers, and of over 30 when calculated according to full-time teaching posts on the Ministry of Education's establishment. The latter is meaningless, inasmuch as primary school teachers normally work a 24-hour week (the number of teaching hours in the lower classes) instead of the standard 30-hour week. The former (26 pupils per teacher) gives 0.85 as the per cent of teachers in the population.
SOURCE: Appendix C.

in developed countries outside Europe (about 27 per cent). Groups I–VI show this effect.

b. The per cent of the 5–19 group attending school rises with income level, from a low rate of one quarter to one half in the underdeveloped countries to a rate of 60 to 80 per cent in the developed countries.

c. The pupil-teacher ratio drops as income level rises, but the trend is less striking, and exists only in the richer country groups.

According to the income level criterion, Israel is an exception in at least two of these three indicators.

a. The 5–19 age-group is 32 per cent of Israel's population, higher than in all European countries and the developed countries of European overseas settlement. The figure is the same as the group IV average. This

TABLE 3.7   *Employment in Education—Israel and the United States*

	United States 1950	Israel Actual 1961	Hypothetical[a] A	B
1. Per cent of population aged 5–19	23.2	32.1	23.2	23.2
2. Per cent of 5–19 age group:				
a. All persons attending educational institutions[b]	85.7	85.8	85.8	85.8
b. Persons attending primary and secondary schools	75.1	72.6	72.6	72.6
3. Per cent of total population:				
a. All persons attending educational institutions (1. × 2a)	19.9	27.5	19.9	19.9
b. Persons attending primary and secondary schools (1. × 2b)	17.3	23.3	16.8	16.8
4. Persons employed in education (thousands)	2,070	53.8	38.8	38.8
5. Number of students[c] per employed person	14.4	11.2	11.2	11.2
6. Labour force[d] participation (per cent)				
a. Of total population	39.6	34.1	34.1	39.6
b. Of working-age population (aged 14 and over)	54.2	51.5		
7. Persons employed in education as per cent of total labour force[d][e]	3.5	7.2	5.2	4.5

[a] A — assuming United States age-structure—i.e. that 23.2 per cent of population are aged 5–19.
B — assuming (in addition to A) the US labour force participation rate of 39.6 per cent of total population.
[b] For Israel, includes 81,000 kindergarten children, some of whom are less than 5 years old; the US figures do not include the under-fives. In both countries persons over 19 receiving higher education are included.
[c] 'Students' refers to all persons covered by item 2a.
[d] Employed civilian labour force.
[e] The total gap between the US and Israel (7.2 *less* 3.5 = 3.7) may be broken down as follows:
  3.7 Total
  2.0 Age-structure (number of children—7.2 *less* 5.2)
  0.5 Age-structure (number of adults) }
  0.2 Labour force participation of working-age population } (5.2 *less* 4.5).
  1.0 Residual effect reflected in pupil-teacher ratio.
See also text, p. 64.
SOURCE: United States—US Bureau of the Census, *Statistical Abstract of the United States, 1953* (various tables) and G. J. Stigler, *Trends in*

Source to Table 3.7 (cont.)

> *Employment in the Service Industries,* NBER Princeton, 1956, p. 11, Table 6.
> Israel—Population: CBS, *SAI 1962,* No. 13, p. 45.
>> School attendance: CBS, *SAI 1963,* No. 14, p. 634.
>> Employment: The LFS estimates underlying Chapter 2 tables. The figure for education employment is 51,800 Jews *plus* an estimate of 2,000 non-Jews derived from the Census.

is of course a reflection of Israel's special demographic structure, with its high proportion of immigrants from oriental countries.

b. The number of pupils per teacher (24 to 26) [27] is among the lowest in the world. Lower rates are found in a number of Western European countries (Sweden, Norway, Austria), but in most of the other developed countries the figure is higher.

c. The rate of school-attendance in the 5–19 group is similar to that of countries at the same income level (group II), and below that of group I. Columns (4) and (5) in the table show calculations based on the first three columns. Column (4) gives the per cent of total population attending school. Column (5), the per cent of teachers in the population, is an index of the education burden imposed on the population. [28] In order to get an index of the education burden imposed on the *adult* population, the effect of demographic structure on labour force participation rates must be taken into account. This is done, in simplified fashion, below.

As could be expected, the high school-attendance rates offset the low percentage of school-age children in the developed countries (and *vice versa* in the underdeveloped countries), so that inter-country differences are much reduced when school-attendance is taken as a per cent of total population. However, the index of education burden is positively, but weakly, correlated with income level.

In Israel, 22.1 per cent of the population attend primary and post-primary school, one of the highest rates in the world, while the burden of education, as here defined, comes to 0.92 according to 24 pupils per teacher, and 0.85 at 26 pupils per teacher. In either case this is the highest rate among the countries for which we found information. This stems partly from objective causes, partly from the high educational standards the country has set itself, and partly from a factor composed of elements of intensity (size of classes, length of the school week etc.).

---

[27] See note e in Table 3.6.
[28] See, however, note d to Table 3.6.

The calculation so far has not taken account of the effect of demo-graphic composition on labour force participation.

Table 3.7 attempts to measure the contribution of each of the above three factors to Israel's high rate of education employment. This was done by a comparison with the appropriate data for the US, which are more detailed than those used in Table 3.6. Here too we see that the 5–19 age-group is a much higher proportion of population in Israel than in the US; that the school-attendance rate is not essentially dif-ferent; and that the employment share of education is higher in Israel. The difference in age-structure explains about 2 percentage points (or over half) of the gap between the education employment shares in Israel and the US. In other words, if the age-structure of Israel were similar to that of the US, 39,000 persons (or 5.2 per cent of employ-ment) would be sufficient, instead of the 54,000 (7.2 per cent of total) actually employed in education in 1961.

The 39,000 employed persons would be only 4.5 per cent of total employment (instead of 5.2 per cent) if labour force participation were the same as in the US [Column (4)]. Part of the 0.7-point difference may also be attributed to age-structure. (See lines 6a and 6b of Table 3.7.) [29] All told, two thirds of the gap between the employment shares of the two countries is explained by demographic differences.

About one third of the gap is explained by differences in the pupil-teacher ratio. In the US there are 14.4 pupils per person engaged in education, compared with 11.2 in Israel—a difference of about 30 per cent in intensity or efficiency of education or both. It is beyond the scope of this work to examine the difference in the number of pupils per teacher, since this would require close study of, *inter alia,* problems of class-size, number of teaching-hours, and number of hours work per teacher.[30]

---

[29] The US labour force participation in total population is about 5.5 percentage points more than in Israel; participation in working-age population (14 and over) is roughly 2.5 percentage points higher in the US. The 3-point dif-ference between these two can also be attributed to the young age-structure of Israel. (See note e to Table 3.7) A more precise calculation requires a long list of additional factors to be taken into account, such as the effect of the reproduction rate on the participation of women in the labour force.

[30] Because of the difficulty of international comparison, we have ignored the problem of the percentage of administrative workers in education. In any case this cannot be of great weight.

4. HEALTH SERVICES

We saw in Chapter 2 that the employment share of health services was much higher in Israel (4.4 per cent) than in the US (3 per cent). If we assume that the employment share of health services is positively correlated with income level, reasons for the divergence must be sought elsewhere. Before attempting to do so we shall extend the comparison made in Chapter 2 to a greater number of countries.

TABLE 3.8   *Selected Health Indicators in Various Countries, by Income Group* [a]

Income Group	Number of persons per doctor [b]		Expectation of Life [c]			
			Men		Women	
I	860	(8)	67.0	(8)	72.0	(8)
II	1,040	(8)	67.7	(7)	72.3	(7)
III	1,260	(5)	60.7	(5)	65.1	(5)
IV	2,280	(11)	49.9	(6)	55.5	(6)
V	3,540	(5)	56.2	(3)	60.3	(3)
VI	3,100	(6)	49.3	(5)	52.4	(5)
VII	10,525	(8)	43.1	(4)	45.5	(4)
Israel	420		70.4		73.6	

[a] The figures in parentheses show the number of countries in each calculation. See also Table 3.6, note b.
[b] The data are for one of the years 1957 through 1960.
[c] Most of the data are for years in the 1950's, and for the late 1940's for a few countries.
SOURCE: Column 1—WHO, *Annual Epidemical and Vital Statistics*, Geneva, 1959, Table 29.1.
    Columns (2) and (3)—UN, *Demographic Yearbook 1961*, Table 5.

Table 3.8 compares the average number of persons per doctor for country income level groups (according to the Kuznets grouping), and shows that the number of persons per doctor declines as income rises. Also striking is the leading position of Israel as the country with the smallest number of persons per doctor (420), no other country approaching this figure. [31]

[31] The corresponding figures for other countries are: Austria and Italy, 620; New Zealand, Switzerland, the Argentine and West Germany—700 to 750; the figure for the US is 790. The ratio 420/790=0.53 is similar to the ratio

Several explanations may be offered. First, a relatively strong demand for health services; the argument that the demand for health services is stronger in Israel than in 'similar' countries rests on three assumptions:

a. The health standards set by the government and other public institutions are very high, especially in comparison with the standards in the countries of origin of many of the new immigrants. In this connexion the initial medical care given to new immigrants must be stressed, as well as extensive activities in preventing epidemic disease, in reducing infant mortality by providing hospital and guidance facilities and cheap or free medical services.

b. The provision of a large part of the health services by public institutions and the sick funds—and not against direct payment—can itself cause demand for health services to rise above the norm. This factor is clearly connected with that discussed in the preceding paragraph.

c. Alongside the demand of the public institutions there may be demand for health services from sections of the community that are particularly sensitive to health problems.

It is difficult to distinguish between these three aspects, nor is it easy to separate them from other demand factors which we shall not discuss here. That they are in fact demand factors may perhaps be deduced from the results achieved by the country's health services. The poor health of many immigrants requires no proof. The results of the health effort can be seen in the elimination or reduction of several endemic diseases, and in the low rate of infant mortality—reflected in the high life expectancy. It would have been difficult to predict, in view of mass immigration, that Israel would today have a life expectancy of 70 for men and 73 for women—rates which compare with those of some Scandinavian countries, and exceed those of most other European countries. [32]

Second, the low efficiency of Israel's health services. The output of health services is conceptually difficult to define and we shall not attempt to clarify the matter here. Nevertheless, in order to discuss the efficiency of health services it is necessary to formulate some—however imprecise—notion of output.

The relatively large number of doctors contrasts with a relative

---

of the employment shares of health services in the two countries: $2.75/4.40 = 0.63$. However, in Israel overconcentration appears to be more marked for doctors than for other medical workers.

[32] See UN, *Demographic Yearbook, 1961*, Table 5.

shortage of hospital facilities. The comparatively small use made of hospitals may entail inefficient health services and overburden the doctor. The situation may be viewed in two, not necessarily exclusive, ways: it may be described as the use of obsolete techniques and production methods in the supply of health services, or we may say that there is production substitutability between modern medical methods requiring more capital, and older methods requiring more doctors. These two hypotheses, separately or combined, may explain the excess employment which co-exists with a marked (no less so than the oversupply of doctors) shortage of hospital facilities. Table 3.9 shows the number of beds per 1,000 population in several countries. Israel, with 5.9 beds per 1,000 (in the early 1950's) lags behind all the countries of Western Europe and Northern America, a lag in facilities which persists today. [33]

TABLE 3.9   *Hospitalization in Selected Countries*[a]

(Number of beds[b] *per 1,000 population)*

India	0.4	Japan	5.5
Iran	0.4	Israel	5.9
Burma	0.5	Lebanon	6.5
Syria	1.1	Netherlands	8.1
Iraq	1.2	Belgium	8.3
Turkey	1.4	Austria	9.9
Egypt	1.6	Italy	9.9
Jordan	1.7	United States	10.1
Spain	2.0	West Germany	10.8
Ceylon	2.7	United Kingdom	11.2
Greece	3.1	France	12.6
Venezuela	3.8	Switzerland	14.0
Yugoslavia	3.9	Denmark	14.0
USSR	4.9	Sweden	14.3

[a] For one of the years 1951 through 1956.
[b] In hospitals for general cases, mental and chronic disease, etc.
SOURCE: *Plan for General Health Insurance in Israel,* Public Committee (Chairman, I. Kanev), 1959, p. 26, Table 50.

Workers in the field are well aware of the shortage; its undesirable results, from the health point of view as well as in terms of efficiency, have been widely discussed. Health services the world over are becoming increasingly dependent on expensive equipment and on methods of

[33] At the end of 1961 there were about 7.2 beds per 1,000 population, just over half of them for general purposes. *(SAI 1963,* No. 14. p. 146.)

treatment requiring hospitalization. The lag in hospital construction means that the doctor must fill the gap, first by inefficient but protracted treatment while the patient waits for admission to hospital, and again, after his premature discharge.

Inefficiency in the supply of health services can also be due to low output of doctors as measured by patients' visits to doctors and doctors' visits to patients. Figures available for 1955 indicate that the number of visits per insured person is somewhat higher in Israel than in other countries, but not sufficiently so to explain the high number of doctors. In 1955, number of visits (patient-to-doctor and doctor-to-patient) per patient was 7.5 in Austria; 5.5 in Italy; 4.8 in Belgium, and 6.1 in Israel. [34] If we multiply these rates by the number of inhabitants per doctor, we find that on the average each doctor made and received visits as follows: Austria—4,650; Italy—3,410; Belgium—3,480; and in Israel only 2,562. [35] No far-reaching conclusions can of course be drawn from this random comparison. Nevertheless, they suggest that Israel's health services suffer from some inefficiency in this sense also.

Third, the source of the supply of doctors. The large number of doctors, the possibility that doctors and hospitals are substitutable, and perhaps the low output (as here defined) of doctors—all combine to raise the question of where the many doctors come from, and of their cost to the community. The answer may lie in the fact that almost all— 91.8 per cent—doctors in the country trained abroad, and arrived in the country with the various waves of immigration and not for economic reasons. [36] This figure should be compared with the percentage of locally trained persons in other professions (32 per cent); this average includes higher figures such as 41.4 per cent for engineers; 50.0 per cent in natural sciences; 53.9 per cent in agriculture; and 34.5 per cent in law. [37] Doctors were on the whole employed in their own profession, (even if there have been complaints about their absorption difficulties

---

[34] See *Plan for General Health Insurance in Israel,* Report of the Public Committee (chairman, I. Kanev), 1959, p. 149, Tables 71 and 72. *SAI 1963,* No. 14, pp. 156–59, gives higher figures.

[35] The number of inhabitants per doctor was taken from the sources of Table 3.8. The figures are not for 1955 but for 1957–1960, and are for total population and not for insured population.

[36] Only a few of the doctors trained abroad came from Israel in the first place.

[37] The data on the per cent of graduates trained in Israel are taken from an (unpublished) 1962 survey of graduates carried out by the CBS.

throughout the period). [38] This suggests, *inter alia,* that there are more than enough foreign-trained doctors to supply the country's needs. These features of Israel's doctor supply were also important in reducing the price of this factor of production. In the first place, the economy saved most of the high cost of training doctors. Second, it can be assumed that the pressure of supply led to a low wage-level for doctors— compared with that of other factors of production required for health (and other) services. Expansion of the hospital system is held back by difficulties in obtaining the necessary funds (principally for maintenance), and by the serious shortage of nurses—perhaps also a budgetary problem. These emphasize even more the relative lowness of the price of doctors.

Both the desire of the economy (i.e., the public sector) to absorb immigrant doctors in their profession and the low price to the economy of doctors encouraged their widespread use: the increase in public demand (and the creation of conditions for increased private demand), and the use of doctors as substitutes for hospitals both reflected the situation.

5. GENERAL GOVERNMENT

We saw in Chapter 2 that general government, and particularly the central government, is an important focus of services overconcentration. In the earlier sections of this chapter we attempted to show that several of the factors affecting the country's industrial structure as a whole have their principal effect in this field. In addition to the import surplus effects, we discussed various aspects of the effect on the number of persons employed in general government of the considerable resources available to or channelled through the public sector (see p. 59). To these we should add:

a. The employment of surplus workers in government institutions as a result of the pressure of unemployment which accompanied mass immigration at various stages; i.e. the creation of disguised unemployment in the civil service. This is largely a legacy of the past, and we shall therefore postpone discussion of it to the historical analysis in Chapter 5.

There are several explanations of general government overconcentration in terms of needs and production conditions.

---

[38] The effect of the occupational structure of immigrants on the industrial structure of the labour force is discussed in Section 3 of Chapter 5.

TABLE 3.10   Civil Servants in Israel and Great Britain

	Great Britain: April 1950				Israel: 31.3.61			
	Thousands	Per cent of labour force[a]	Per cent of total (in each panel)	Per million inhabitants	Thousands	Per cent of labour force[a]	Per cent of total (in each panel)	Per million inhabitants
A. Total civil service and police	1,151.7	4.99	100.0	22,804	48.210	6.23	100.0	22,128
Defence—civilian employees	390.8	1.69	33.9	7,737	1.264	0.16	2.6	580
Classification adjustment[b]	–	–	–	–	9.208	1.19	19.1	4,226
PTT	321.8	1.39	28.0	6,371	7.773	1.01	16.1	3,568
All other departments	439.1	1.91	38.1	8,696	29.965	3.87	62.2	13,754
B. All other departments[c]	439.1	1.91	100.0	8,696	29.965	3.87	100.0	13,754
Administration and police	157.5	0.70	35.9	3,119	15.548	2.01	51.9	7,137
Police and prisons	75.4	0.34	17.2	1,493	7.666	0.99	25.6	3,519
Home affairs	4.0	0.01	0.9	79	0.635	0.08	2.1	292
Other administrative departments[d]	14.1	0.07	3.2	279	2.977	0.39	9.9	1,366
Revenue departments	64.0	0.28	14.6	1,268	4.270	0.55	14.3	1,960
Foreign relations	10.1	0.04	2.3	200	0.739	0.10	2.5	339
Foreign	6.2	0.03	1.4	123	0.739	0.10	2.5	339
Colonial	3.9	0.01	0.9	77	–	–	–	–
Social services	73.9	0.32	16.8	1,464	5.801	0.75	19.3	2,663
Education	3.3	0.01	0.8	65	1.527	0.20	5.1	701
Health	5.9	0.03	1.3	117	1.482	0.19	4.9	680

Welfare	8.5	0.04	1.9	169	1.090	0.14	3.6	501
Housing	1.3	0.00	0.3	26	0.548	0.07	1.8	252
National insurance	46.0	0.20	10.5	911	0.807	0.10	2.7	370
Others[c]	8.9	0.04	2.0	176	0.347	0.05	1.2	159
Economic services	*128.0*	*0.55*	*29.2*	*2,535*	*5.129*	*0.66*	*17.1*	*2,354*
Agriculture	30.9	0.13	7.0	612	1.850	0.24	6.2	849
Trade, industry, development	47.3	0.21	10.8	937	1.167	0.15	3.9	536
Transport	14.4	0.06	3.3	285	0.884	0.11	2.9	406
Labour	29.9	0.13	6.8	592	0.422	0.06	1.4	194
Scientific research	2.9	0.01	0.7	58	0.160	0.02	0.5	73
Other	2.6	0.01	0.6	51	0.646	0.08	2.2	296
Ancillary agencies	*59.8*	*0.26*	*13.6*	*1,184*	*2.748*	*0.35*	*9.2*	*1,261*
Survey department	4.6	0.02	1.0	91	0.391	0.05	1.3	179
Public works	46.1	0.20	10.5	913	1.933	0.25	6.5	887
Printing and publishing	9.1	0.04	2.1	180	0.424	0.05	1.4	195
Miscellaneous employees	*9.8*	*0.04*	*2.2*	*194*				

[a] Total labour force in Great Britain; civilian labour force in Israel.

[b] Government of Israel employees engaged in functions not carried out by the central government in Great Britain. Includes President's and Knesset secretariats; courts of justice; broadcasting services; employees of railways and Haifa and Eilat ports; employees of Ministry of Health hospitals.

[c] The figures for the two countries have been made comparable as far as possible. The item descriptions are functional rather than departmental.

[d] Includes also some administrative sections of ministries whose main function is classified under other items of the table.

[e] War damage compensation in Great Britain, and Ministry of Religions in Israel.

SOURCE: Great Britain—M. Abramovitz and V. F. Eliasberg, *The Growth of Public Employment in Great Britain*, NBER, Princeton 1957, pp. 40–45, Table 4, and p. 70, Table 8.
Israel—Civil Service Commission, *Eleventh Report 1960/61*, p. 86, Table B.1 (Hebrew).

b. The conception of the role of government and economic needs: throughout the years of its existence the Israel economy has been run by a social democratic party, with a very broad conception of the functions of government. The conditions prevailing in the country since the establishment of the State, in particular the burden of absorbing immigrants undertaken by the country and the defence burden imposed on it by others, justify this ideology, and even accentuate it. Clearly, Israel is one of the countries in which the ideological factor is apt to raise the optimum budget above its normal level. [39] This factor, whose effects we have already seen in our discussion of education and health, is, as it were, the obverse of the resource effect.

c. The export of government services: the activities of the national institutions abroad in Jewish affairs generally, and in education and culture in the Diaspora, is sometimes considered an export of general government services.

d. Inefficiency in general government: the argument that government services are less efficient than other economic branches is old and well-known. But before such an explanation of overconcentration can be accepted the relative efficiency of general government in Israel must be compared with that in other countries, and this is difficult. Nevertheless, we shall attempt to draw some conclusions on one aspect of this problem, raised mainly by Kuznets—the existence of economies of scale in the provision of a considerable part of government services. Specifically, in a small country a higher proportion of the labour force (and resources) must be employed to produce a given volume of government services than in a large country. [40]

Table 3.10 makes a detailed comparison of the composition of the civil services of Israel (1961) and Great Britain (1950). The UK had the highest proportion of product originating in government (35 per cent) of all the countries in Oshima's study.[41] We are here comparing two governments whose approach is similar, and who have a similar proportion of the country's resources at their disposal. If considerable

---

[39] See the discussion in Section 2, pp. 53 ff.

[40] S. Kuznets, "Economic Growth of Small Nations," in *Economic Consequences of the Size of Nations,* (ed. E.A.G. Robinson), London, 1960, pp. 14–32.

[41] This is evidence of the well-known facts of the UK government's approach (and especially that of the post-war Labour government) to the functions of government in general, and to the provision of services through the public sector in particular. The matter is also discussed in M. Abramovitz and V.F. Eliasberg, *The Growth of Public Employment in Great Britain,* NBER, Princeton, 1957, *passim.*

differences in size exist between the two civil services that are not due to institutional factors we may conclude that the ideological and the resource factors are not the only ones affecting the size of Israel's government services.

The data of Table 3.10 refer to all central government employees, (i.e. not only to those classified under general government in our classification) and they include persons engaged in other services (health, transportation) and in other industries (manufacturing, agriculture, etc.) if they are employed by the central government. The comparison between the two countries of course raises several problems connected with institutional differences and the allocation of functions to different governmental authorities. In order to solve the most important of these problems we have (in Panel A of the table) segregated civilians employed in defence in both countries, as well as a number of civil servants in Israel carrying out functions which are in the UK carried out by nationalized public corporations. [42] PTT employees in both countries were also classed separately. The employment share of this branch (which belongs to transportation), is smaller in Israel than in Great Britain according to all the criteria of Table 3.10: in Israel the figure is 1 per cent of employed labour force, compared with 1.4 per cent in Great Britain, and there is a still greater difference when the figures are expressed per million inhabitants. The share of PTT in government is also higher in Great Britain than in Israel. These differences can stem from the scope of the service and from the degree of efficiency and mechanization, as well as from objective factors such as the distribution and density of the population. [43]

In 1950, about 440,000 persons (or 1.9 per cent of labour force) were employed in the administrative system of the civilian departments in the British government. The corresponding figure for Israel is 30,000, which is 3.9 per cent of civilian labour force, or double the percentage in Great Britain. When expressed in civil servants per million population,

---

[42] About 270,000 (or over two thirds) of the civilian defence employees in the UK are 'industrial staff' and are engaged in the operation of military installations and in various military industries. Differences in the allocation of functions to civilian or military personnel in the two armies do not permit comparison of this item.

[43] M. Abramovitz and V.F. Eliasberg, *op. cit.*, pp. 54, 58, discuss the efficiency lag in the British postal services in 1945–50, when the number of workers rose by 26 per cent without any clear evidence of expanded activity, as a result of reductions in working hours. The lag can also be seen in the PTT column of Table 3.11.

the gap is slightly smaller. [44] This is partly due to the fact that in Israel the central government carries out several functions which are in the UK carried out by other government agencies. In particular, border guards are included in police in Israel, and some of the administrative functions of the Israel Ministry of Health are in Great Britain carried out by the National Health Service Board; moreover educational services are mostly the business of the local authorities in Great Britain. All these together can explain at most 0.5 percentage points of the gap, which still leaves a difference of 1.5 percentage points, or 80 per cent, between the two countries. Table 3.10 brings out the following points.

a. Most of the gap between the two countries is concentrated in general services and police, and in foreign relations. Absolutely, the largest gap is in 'police and prisons' (and it should be remembered that the Israel figure includes the border police), but considerable relative differences exist in every item, whether in the revenue units of the Treasury, or in foreign relations, a field in which the UK has far greater responsibilities than Israel. Whether the comparison is in terms of the percentage of labour force or per million inhabitants does not affect the picture.

b. There is a much smaller gap in employment in economic services and in ancillary agencies (which are also mainly economic). The British figures for economic services per million inhabitants exceed those of Israel.

c. The employment share of welfare services in Israel is double the British figure. A large part of the gap is apparently due to differences in definition, but this is not sufficient explanation.

The same conclusions are more strikingly shown by the internal composition of civil servants (excluding PTT) in the two countries. In Israel over 50 per cent of civil servants work in general administration and police, compared with only 40 per cent in Great Britain where the majority are engaged in economic and welfare services.

Do these differences show that in Israel the government provides a greater supply of services, or that the civil service is less efficient (in the senses discussed above)? There is no unambiguous answer to this question. The considerable gap in general administration and the much

---

[44] The difference between the two calculations (1.5:1, instead of 2:1) is due to the fact that the civilian labour force participation rate (of total population) in Israel is lower than the total labour force participation rate in Great Britain.

TABLE 3.11   *Central Government Employees in Selected Countries*

	Population (millions)	Central government employees				
		Thousands	Per thousand inhabitants			
			Total	Finance	PTT	Foreign affairs
	(1)	*(2)*	*(3)*	*(4)*	*(5)*	*(6)*
India (30.6.60)	431.7	821	1.9	..	..	..
United States (30.6.62)	186.5	1,466	7.9	0.45	3.16	0.21
Japan (1.10.61)	93.3	651	7.0	0.72	3.13	0.03
United Kingdom (1.4.62)	52.9	1,089	20.6	1.38	6.86	0.19
France (1956)	43.6	1,102	25.3	3.01	5.48	0.09
Netherlands (31.12.60)	11.5	216	18.8	1.83	4.96	0.20
Australia (30.6.61)	10.5	165	15.7	1.05	8.29	0.11
Sweden (1960)	7.5	235	31.3	0.80	4.53	0.15
Switzerland (1959)	5.3	104	19.7	..	6.80	..
Norway (1962)	3.6	39	10.8	..	..	..
Ireland (April 1961)	2.8	39	13.9	..	..	..
New Zealand (31.3.61)	2.4	62	25.8	1.38	..	..
Israel (31.3.63)	2.3	50	21.7	2.78	3.91	0.35

SOURCE: Israel—Civil Service Commission, *Thirteenth Report, 1962/63,* 1963, p. 157, Table A.1 (Hebrew).
Other countries—National sources (statistical abstracts, civil service commission reports, etc.).
Population figures from UN, *Demographic Yearbook,* several issues.

smaller gap in welfare and economic services suggest the second explanation.

To what extent are differences in efficiency due to diseconomies of scale of Israel's government services? To answer this question, the argument must first be formulated and given theoretical and empirical foundation. The theoretical grounds for the existence of diseconomies of scale may be stated in two ways:

First, the scope of some government services is primarily a function of the existence of an independent political unit, and only secondarily of its size. This is so, for example, in a prime minister's office, the legislature, the foreign office, and some economic planning services.

Second, some government services have, like private enterprises, an optimum size, which is reached only in countries much larger than Israel. Examples are the administration of economic services, health, education, revenue collection, etc.

It is more difficult to provide empirical proof of these hypotheses. Attempts made to examine this factor from the government outlay side have not provided any *prima facie* confirmation. We have tried to approach the problem from the point of view of employment in government services in countries of varying size; however, it became clear that the problem requires thorough study in its own right.

Table 3.11 brings a few of the relevant figures for a small number of countries, covering a wide size range. We chose the number of inhabitants as the variable indicating size. The table is not very helpful since it enables us to distinguish only between the three largest countries and all the others. In other words, if there are diseconomies of scale, they are not visible in the data for the 2 to 50 million inhabitants category. This conclusion emerges both from the figures for total employees [column (3)] and those for specific government departments [columns (4) to (6)]. In any case, the difference between the three largest countries and the rest may be explained in widely varying ways. Even if this difference is due to scale effects, these cannot explain the differences between Israel and other countries, most of which have populations of up 50 million.

6. SUMMARY

a. To the points discussed in detail in the chapter, the following must be added:

   i. The occupational structure of immigrants has been briefly discussed above in connexion with the supply of doctors (see pp.

68–69. It seems unlikely that—except for doctors—this factor has
had any marked effect on economic structure in recent years
(see Chapter 5, Section 3).

ii.   The overestimate of personal services owing to the inclusion of
      kibbutz services (see Table 4.6).
iii. The relatively large number of welfare workers, which un-
      doubtedly stems from the needs of mass immigration.
iv.   An additional factor mentioned in the literature and which may
      affect industrial structure is implicit in a system of price controls
      imposed on goods but not on services. Such a system has been
      intermittently in effect in various forms since the beginning of
      the second world war.[45] In this study we shall not enter into
      an analysis of its possible effects, but confine ourselves to remark-
      ing that this also entails no decline in the product-worker ratio.
v.   The discussion in this chapter referred to the whole population.
      For the Jewish sector by itself we find an even higher share of
      employment devoted to services in general and to public services
      in particular (Tables 2.2 and 4.5), and it should be remembered
      that various services are supplied by the Jewish to the Arab
      sector.

b.   The factors analysed in the chapter almost fully explain the
overconcentration in services in Israel. Most important are the various
import surplus and foreign trade effects which, when taken at their
upper limits, may explain most of the excess.[46] If all other supply and
demand conditions for goods and services were the same in Israel as
in other countries at the same income level, a 6 per cent excess services
employment could be expected. In fact, other conditions do differ, and
explain some of the remaining gap: the considerable resources at the
disposal of the public sector, which are likely to affect the economy's
choice between goods and services; the high health, education, and
administrative requirements, which also—in a different sense—operate
from the demand side; on the supply side, and of much less importance,
there is the relatively large supply of doctors, and perhaps also some
inefficiency and disguised unemployment in government institutions.

c.   Evidently there is a close connexion between the import surplus
effects and the overconcentration of employment and financial resources

[45] This is mentioned in connexion with the early years of the State by M.
Michaely, *op. cit.*

[46] The import surplus income and substitution effects and the foreign trade
effect can account for 10 to 15 percentage points of the 12 to 16 per cent gap.

in education, health, and administration. We have already seen that the import surplus is an important source of finance for these services.

The assumption hitherto and in what follows is that the size of the import surplus is independent of the country's needs, when 'needs' stands for most of the import surplus effects mentioned in this chapter. This assumption is at best an approximation. The causal connexion between the country's needs and the import surplus undoubtedly works both ways: clearly, needs influence the size of the import surplus, and thus constitute the ultimate cause of some of the import surplus effects. Services requirements are, however, not the only ones demanding an import surplus, and this partly, though not wholly, justifies treating the import surplus as exogenous.

d. If these do in fact explain the overconcentration of employment in services, the product-worker ratio cannot be expected to drop below the normal level—the conclusion reached in Chapter 2. Apart from the last two, not very important, factors in paragraph (b), all the explanations are in terms of a particularly heavy demand for services, and it follows that none of them is likely to reduce the services product-worker ratio. There may be some tendency for the ratio to decline in general government and perhaps in medical services where supply factors have greater weight. Nevertheless, it must again be stressed that there is no necessary connexion between the wage level and actual output in general government, so that a wage rate may prevail which is not consistent with disguised unemployment or inefficiency.[47] It should also be borne in mind that the government is to a large extent a pace-setter in clerical wages, and for other public services.

[47] See the related discussion in Chapter 2, pp. 15 and 37.

Chapter 4: The Development of the Service Industries: 1931-1961

1. PALESTINE AND ISRAEL

Domestic product

The first national income estimates for Palestine were made by A.L. Gaathon for 1936.[1] Additional estimates of the industrial origin of national income, for the Jewish and non-Jewish sectors separately, were made by Loftus[2] for 1944 and 1945. For the period of the State, we have Gaathon's estimates for the Jewish sector for 1950 and 1951,[3] as well as the revised 12-year series prepared by the NAD, which includes the Arab sector. Tables 4.1 and 4.2 summarize the data for selected years.[4]

The most noticeable feature of the series is that the beginning and end of period figures differ only slightly in 'all services'—46.1 and 49.4[5] per cent in 1936 and 1961, respectively. In the interim, however, there were fluctuations, and the product share of services declined from 1936 to 1945 and rose from 1945 to 1952;[6] there has been no change in the last ten years. For the second period, at least, part of the change can be ascribed to the establishment of the State and its concomitants—in particular the transfer of all government functions to the Jewish sector. An explanation of the results may be sought in a separate discussion of each service branch (Tables 4.2 to 4.4).

The changes were reflected in the internal structure of services (see Table 4.2, Panel A): the shares of transportation and personal services

---

[1] L. Gruenbaum (Gaathon), *National Income and Outlay in Palestine 1936*, Jerusalem, 1941.

[2] P.J. Loftus, *National Income of Palestine 1944*, Government Printer, 1946, and *National Income of Palestine 1945*, Government Printer, 1948.

[3] A.L. Gaathon, *Survey of Israel's Economy 1951*, FP and CBS Technical Paper 1, Jerusalem, 1959.

[4] It is worth nothing here that, for the sake of consistency, public utilities have been excluded from services in all the historical series, except for municipal waterworks and sanitary services, which are included in general government (under local authorities).

[5] If the Arab sector is excluded from the 1961 data, the figure will be slightly higher.

[6] For 1951, about 5 per cent must be deducted from 'all services' for ownership of dwellings. Other comments on 1951 are made later.

TABLE 4.1   Net Product[a] in Palestine[b] and Israel: Selected Years

(per cent)

	1936	1945	1951	1952	1955	1959	1961 (II)[c]	1961 (I)[c]
A. Total	100.0	100.0	100.0	100.0	100.0	100.0	100.0	100.0
Agriculture	9.7	10.2	7.3	11.5	11.2	11.9	10.9	10.9
Industry	20.2	38.7	23.9	23.2	23.4	23.5	24.7	24.7
Construction	9.3	4.6	10.3	9.0	8.1	7.3	7.2	7.3
Ownership of dwellings	12.2	4.0	..[e]	5.3	5.4	5.6	5.8	5.8
Public utilities	2.5[d]	..[e]	..[e]	1.6	1.6	2.1	2.0	2.6
Services	46.1	42.5	58.5	49.4	50.3	49.6	49.4	48.7
B. Services	46.1	42.5	58.5[f]	49.4	50.3	49.6	49.4	48.7
Transportation	6.6	6.5	8.6[g]	7.0	6.9	7.4	7.3	7.5
Commerce	25.7	17.8	17.2	14.9	14.2	14.1	14.8	14.9
Trade	20.8[h]	..	13.8	12.6	11.7	11.2	11.2	11.2
Finance	4.9	..	3.4	2.3	2.5	2.9	3.6	3.7
Public services	9.1	13.0	21.6	21.1	23.2	22.7	22.0	21.0
General government	4.9	7.9[i]	12.5[g]	..	..	..	10.5	9.5
Other public services	4.2[j]	5.1	9.1	..	..	..	11.5	11.5
Personal services	4.7[k]	5.2	11.1[f]	6.4	6.0	5.4	5.3	5.3
C. Total in millions of LP or IL	17.2	78.6	527.7	843.5	1,784.1	3,221.5	4,318.1	4,318.1

a 1936, 1945 and 1951—NNP. Other years—NDP.   b Jewish sector only.

c Variant I: the source data have been adjusted as far as possible to conform to the labour force classification.
Variant II: incorporates only those adjustments which can easily be made for the earlier years as well.
This notation is also used in subsequent tables.

d Power generation only.   e Included in industry.   f Includes elements of ownership of dwellings.

g PTT is included in general government.   h Includes restaurants, cafes, and kiosks.

i Includes LP 1.8 million (2.3 per cent) paid to Jewish members of the armed forces.   j See note k.

k Includes a small amount of public services; see also note h.

SOURCE: 1936—L. Gruenbaum (Gaathon), National Income and Outlay in Palestine 1936, Jerusalem, 1941.
1945—P. J. Loftus, National Income of Palestine 1945, Government Printer, 1948.
1951—A.L. Gaathon, Survey of Israel's Economy, 1951, FP and CBS, Technical Paper No. 1, 1959.
1952–61—NAD, adjusted in order to obtain as consistent a series as possible. See Appendix B.

TABLE 4.2   *The Composition of Net Product Originating in Services: Selected Years*

	1936 (per cent of total net product)	1936	1945	1952	1961 II
A. *Per cent of total services*					
Services	**100.0**	**100.0**	**100.0**	**100.0**
Transportation	14.4	15.3	14.2	14.8
Commerce	55.7	41.9	30.1	29.9
Trade	*45.0*	..	*25.5*	*22.7*
Finance	*10.7*	..	*4.6*	*7.2*
Public services	19.8	30.5	42.7	44.6
General government	*10.7*	*18.5*	..	*21.2*
Other public services	*9.1*	*12.0*	..	*23.4*
Personal services	10.1	12.3	13.0	10.7
B. *The share of services in total net product—index (1936=100)*					
Services	**46.1**	100.0	92.1	107.1	107.0
Transportation	6.6	100.0	97.7	106.0	109.8
Commerce	25.7	100.0	69.4	57.8	57.5
Trade	*20.8*	100.0	..	60.6	53.9
Finance	*4.9*	100.0	..	45.9	72.6
Public services	9.1	100.0	141.9	230.5	240.5
General government	*4.9*	100.0	160.0	..	212.6
Other public services	*4.2*	100.0	120.6	..	273.0
Personal services	*4.7*	100.0	112.0	138.2	114.0

SOURCE: See sources to Table 4.1.

remained constant, but there was a steep decline in the share of trade (from 45 to 23 per cent of services product), and of finance, while the share of public services rose from 20 to 45 per cent of services product. *Transportation:* The product share of this branch rose from 6.6 per cent at the beginning of the period to 7.3 per cent in 1961, or by 10 per cent, somewhat more than the share of services as a whole (see Table 4.2). Not too much weight should be given to these figures because of the small absolute size of the branch. The rise begins after 1945, and was apparently held back before this by the wartime shortage of vehicles and fuel. [7] Within transportation (Table 4.3), we see the

[7] The 1952 figures suggest that Gaathon's 1951 estimate is too high (Table 4.1).

TABLE 4.3   *Net Product Originating in Transportation:*
             Selected Years

(per cent)

	1936	1945	1952	1955	1959	1961 II
A. Share in total product						
Total [a]	6.6	6.5	7.0	6.9	7.4	7.3
Railways	0.5	..	0.6	0.4	0.4	0.3
Road transportation	5.5	..	3.5	3.6	3.8	3.8
Shipping and aviation	–	..	2.0	2.0	2.3	2.3
PTT	0.6	..	0.9	0.9	0.9	0.9
B. Per cent of transportation						
Total [a]	100.0	100.0	100.0	100.0	100.0	100.0
Railways	8.0	..	8.1	6.0	4.6	4.6
Road transportation	82.6	..	50.5	51.4	51.0	50.7
Shipping and aviation	–	..	27.9	29.1	31.6	31.9
PTT	9.4	..	13.5	13.5	12.8	12.8
C. Share in total product—index [b] (1936=100)						
Total	100	98	106	104	111	110
Railways	100	..	107	77	64	64
Road transportation	100	..	65	64	68	67
PTT	100	..	153	150	152	150

[a] In millions of LP or IL: 1.1   5.1   59.4   122.9   237.6   314.8.
[b] Calculated from unrounded figures underlying panel A.
SOURCE: See Table 4.1.

rapid emergence of shipping and aviation, in which the Jewish sector had almost no part in the 1930's, and a decline in the share of inland transportation—both roads and railways—as a per cent of both transportation and total product.

Commerce: There has been a sharp decline of about 50 per cent [8] in the product share of trade. Most of the decline occurred during the mandatory period (as may be seen from the 1945 commerce figure) but it continued more slowly also throughout the period of the State. [9]

[8] In 1936, trade apparently includes restaurants and cafes (as distinct from hotels)—about 1 to 2 per cent of total. A negligible amount of shipping is also included.

[9] It should here be noted that Gaathon's figures for product originating in services in 1951 seem to be too high, especially when we compare them to the 1952 figure from the NAD series (Table 4.1). The remaining divergences apparently stem from differences in measurement and methods.

TABLE 4.4   *Net Product Originating in Trade: 1952, 1955 and 1959*

(per cent)

	1952	1955	1959
A. Total trade	100.0	100.0	100.0
Wholesale trade	33.9	40.7	38.8
Retail trade	66.1	59.3	61.2
B. Food retail trade as per cent of total retail trade	..	41.5	40.9
C. Total trade in millions of IL	106.1	208.0	360.5

SOURCE: See Table 4.1.

Finance, which includes banks, credit societies and real estate firms, does not show any consistent trend. From 1952 on there is a continuous increase in the share of this sub-branch, a rise which may have begun as early as 1945. Nevertheless, the 1936 figure is higher than that for 1961. The high 1936 level may be explained historically by the fact that this was a peak year for capital transfers to the country and that the financial field was considerably expanded as a result of immigration from central Europe. Here also, the reliability of the data is affected by the small size of the branch.

The share of all the distributive services in product declined considerably over the period, despite the rise in transportation.

Public services: The product share of this group of services—supplied for the most part by the public sector—rose from 9 to 22 per cent over the period, or by 140 per cent (see Tables 4.1 and 4.2). This is the highest increase found and, in fact, underlies the moderate rise in the share of 'all services.' Most of the increase took place between 1945 and 1951. In other words, the establishment of the State was undoubtedly the principal direct cause of the jump in the share of these services. This stands in contrast to the subsequent period, when the public services product share remained constant.

There was however some upward tendency from 1936 to 1945, a tendency which is more prominent in the employment figures. The transfer of authority at the time of partition imposed on the Jewish sector the burden of supplying services—some of which had previously been received from a government in which the sector participated to only a small extent. [10] The change of regime was accompanied by a change in the conceptions of government functions, and this also extended the scope of government activity, all the more so because of the immediate requirements of mass immigration. Moreover, national defence devolved on the Jewish sector and its character and scope changed markedly owing to the persistent threat of war.

As stated, the product share of public services rose from 1936 to 1945. The general government component continued to rise thereafter, from 5.6 [11] per cent in 1945 to 10.5 per cent in 1961, partly because of the above-mentioned transfer of defence responsibilities.

The product share of 'other public services' especially education and health, went up even more steeply, from 5.1 per cent in 1945 to 11.5 per cent in 1961. Again, most of the increase occurred with the transfer from Mandatary to State. During the mandatory period there were apparently no great changes, and it is possible that the share of product originating in this branch dropped somewhat from 1936 to 1945. [12]

Personal services: Tables 4.1 and 4.2 show that the product share of personal services was in 1961 somewhat higher than in 1936. In between, the share rose until 1952 and declined thereafter. If we take into account the 1–2 per cent of product of restaurants and cafes which were not included in the 1936 figure, we see that there was in fact a decline from 1936 to 1961. [13] The decline since the establishment of the State is accounted for by the items 'personal and municipal services in kibbutzim' and 'domestic services'; there was however a slight rise in the share of hotel and entertainment services. [14]

Other branches: The principal changes in non-service branches were as follows: the product share of Jewish sector agriculture stayed throughout at around 9 to 10 per cent. [15] Manufacturing raised its product share by 22 per cent from 1936 to 1961. The branch grew considerably

---

[10] The Jewish sector product originating in government services is equal to the salaries of Jewish civil servants and police. See Table 5.3, p. 116.

[11] The figure in Table 4.1 (7.9 per cent) includes 2.3 per cent—LP 1.8 million —paid to Jewish members of the British armed forces.

[12] In 1936, health and educational services accounted for about 4 per cent of national income, compared with 5.1 per cent (all other public services) in 1945. In 1961, health and education services were 7.9 per cent of product.

[13] In 1961, personal services include 1.8 per cent for this item, without which the share of personal services comes to 3.5 per cent.

[14] According to the NAD series.

[15] The higher figures shown in Table 4.1 for the period of the State are due to the importance of the non-Jewish sector in agriculture.

during, and because of, the second world war, but subsequently contracted during the later years of the Mandate and the early years of the State, to expand once more in recent years. Construction, affected by war and variations in immigration, showed wide fluctuations. The share of ownership of dwellings dropped steeply from 1936 to 1945, when it was below the level of the 1950's. This drop is certainly connected both with the housing shortage of the 1936 benchmark and with the control measures introduced at the beginning of the war.[16]

Employed persons

The employment series covers a longer period than the product data, the starting point being the 1931 census of population; moreover, there is a greater number of employment estimates covering the mandatory and early State period. The estimates were produced by different institutions using a variety of methods. The 1931 data are based on the mandatory government's population census; those for 1936 are Gaathon's estimates; the other estimates for the mandatory period are based mainly on figures of the Jewish Agency's Statistical Department, which in turn were based on censuses for single branches. Apart from the two population censuses (1948 and 1961) carried out since the establishment of the State, there are the estimates of the industrial structure of earners made by A. Nizan for 1947–52, which were based *inter alia* on the 1948 population census and on a 1950 labour force enumeration. The second part of the State period, from 1954, is covered by the CBS Labour Force Surveys (LFS)—for these, the number of surveys carried out in each year rose over the period.

The definition of the unit of investigation differed from source to source. During the mandatory period and until the LFS were initiated, the usual definition of 'earner' included persons living on dividends, pensions, foreign transfers, and even on charity. The LFS introduced the concept of 'employed person' which included only persons receiving earned income. Here also, the definition of 'earned income recipient' is not uniform throughout the period.

In the LFS, 'employed person' as distinct from 'unemployed' is defined as a person aged 14 and over who was employed for at least one hour [17] in the survey week. The mandatory estimates usually required

---

[16] Apropos of our subsequent international comparisons, it should here be mentioned that when ownership of dwellings is included in services there is a net decline in the share of product originating in services over the period.

[17] With the minor exception of 'unpaid members of family' for whom the minimum is 15 hours.

a longer determining period. In the LFS and in the 1961 census both part-time and full-time workers were counted as employed persons, while in some of the earlier estimates attempts were made to convert figures for part-time workers into a suitable full-time equivalent. [18] These differences in the length of the determining period exist also for the definition of the employed person's branch and occupation. We will not discuss the changes in industrial classification that took place over the period.

It was not possible to reconcile many of the differences, and we concentrated mainly on the more relevant adjustments: (a) the inclusion of part-time workers (including unpaid members of families); (b) the exclusion of income recipients who are not 'employed persons'; (c) an attempt to achieve uniformity in industrial classification. It was, however, found impossible to make a reliable breakdown of Nizan's 1947–52 figures into 'employed' and 'non-employed' income recipients, and these data are therefore presented without adjustment. This to a large extent vitiates any attempt to evaluate developments, especially in commerce, during the early years of the State. [19]

Tables 4.5 to 4.7 show the figures for Palestine and Israel from 1931–61. For comparison, Table 4.5 also shows figures for the whole population. According to the censuses which open and close our period, the share of services in Jewish employment rose from 45.4 per cent to 53.3 per cent, or by 17 per cent (Table 4.5). The corresponding figure from the 1948 Registration of Population lies between these two, and, on the face of it, shows a rising trend throughout the period. However, other estimates for 1961 and for the intervening years, and a closer examination of the figures themselves give a different picture of both the extent and the continuity of the changes. Panel C of Table 4.6 gives the employment share of services excluding persons employed in personal services in kibbutzim (first included in the data in 1939). [20] The change between the two censuses is somewhat smaller than before

---

[18] Thus, for example, the estimate of agricultural employment made by the Jewish Agency. See Jewish Agency, "The Occupational Structure of Jewish Earners," *Alon Statisti,* Vol. I, Nos. 1–6, June 1946, p. 17.

[19] A tentative adjustment of the Nizan data showed a branch structure of employed persons which does not differ markedly from that of 1948 or 1954–55 (LFS). In particular, it does not differ from the latter in the per cent employed in all services and in commerce. (See source to Table 4.6).

[20] For the mandatory period from 1939 the kibbutz figures were estimated by the author, and from 1948 on by the compilers of the various surveys and censuses.

TABLE 4.5   *Employed Persons by Industry in Palestine and Israel: 1931, 1948 and 1961*

(*per cent*)

	Total Population		Jews		
	1931	1961	1931	1948	1961
Total in thousands	293.3	709.8	65.7	311.8	656.3
A. Total	**100.0**	**100.0**	**100.0**	**100.0**	**100.0**
Agriculture	55.3	14.1	22.1	14.2	11.9
Industry [e]	12.1	25.7	23.8	31.8	26.5
Construction	4.7	8.8	8.7	6.1	8.3
Services	27.9	51.4	45.4	47.9	53.3
B. Services	**27.9**	**51.4**	**45.4**	**47.9**	**53.3**
Transportation	*5.5*	*6.5*	*5.5*	*6.2*	*6.7*
Commerce	*8.8*	*12.3*	*14.1*	*13.3*	*12.7*
Trade	8.4	9.7	12.9	11.9	9.9
Finance	0.4	2.6	1.2	1.4	2.8
Public services	*7.2*	*25.5*	*15.2*	*18.9*	*26.6*
General government [a][c]	2.3	10.7	2.1	7.7	11.2
Education [b]	1.9	7.0	5.8	4.7	7.2
Health	1.1	4.1	3.1	3.9	4.4
Other community services	1.9	3.7	4.2	2.6	3.8
Personal services [d]	*6.4*	*7.1*	*10.6*	*9.5*	*7.3*
Domestic services	3.6	2.3	5.8	2.3	2.5
Catering services	1.5	2.8	2.1	2.4	2.8
Other personal services	1.3	2.0	2.7	4.8	2.0

[a] Of which, police   1.2   1.1   0.8   0.9   1.1.
[b] Education excluding Yeshivot   1.6   6.5   4.3   ..   6.7.
[c] Electricity and national water supply in industry; municipal waterworks and sanitary services in general government.
[d] In 1931 kibbutz services are not included; in 1948 they are included in other personal services (2.8 per cent of Total); in 1961 kibbutz services are allocated to the various items.
The figure for dining services (in catering) is 0.7 per cent of Total.
SOURCE: 1931—E. Mills, *Census of Palestine 1931,* Vol. 1, Government of Palestine, 1933.
                  1948—CBS, *Registration of Population (8.XI.1948) Part B,* Special Series No. 53, (Hebrew), pp. 36–41.
                  1961—See Table 2.3.

TABLE 4.6   Jewish Employed Persons: Selected Years[a]

(per cent)

	1931	1936	1939	1943	1945	1947[b]	1948	1951[b]	1954	1955	1959	1961 (1)	1961 (2)
A. Total	100.0	100.0	100.0	100.0	100.0	100.0	100.0	100.0	100.0	100.0	100.0	100.0	100.0
Agriculture	22.1	21.4	20.8	14.0	13.4	12.6	14.2	13.8	14.7	15.0	14.2	14.5	11.9
Industry[c]	23.8	20.1	21.3	31.4	31.1	26.5	31.8	23.6	24.5	23.7	25.6	25.6	26.5
Construction	8.7	9.4	7.9	9.6	4.9	8.7	6.1	9.5	9.2	9.1	9.2	8.5	8.3
Services	45.4	49.1	50.0	45.0	50.6	52.2	47.9	53.1	51.6	52.2	51.0	51.4	53.3
B. Services	45.4	49.1	50.0	45.0	50.6	52.2	47.9	53.1	51.6	52.2	51.0	51.4	53.3
Transportation	5.5	5.3	5.6	4.5	5.1	6.3	6.2	7.0	6.7[d]	6.4	6.8	6.7	6.7
Commerce	14.1	15.7	14.6	12.2	14.7	19.4	13.3	16.8	13.1	14.0	12.4	12.3	12.7
Trade	12.9	14.0	12.9	10.7	13.3	..	11.9	..	11.6	..	..	10.0	9.9
Finance	1.2	1.7	1.7	1.5	1.4	..	1.4	..	1.5	..	..	2.3	2.8
Public services	15.2	18.1	20.2	17.3	20.8	18.6[e]	18.9	18.2[e]	21.8	23.1	24.0	25.0	26.6
General government	2.1	6.7	6.4	8.5[f]	7.6	7.9	7.7	10.3	8.6	..	9.5	9.4	11.2
Other public services	13.1	11.4	13.8	8.8	13.2	10.7	11.2	7.9	13.2	..	14.5	15.6	15.4
Personal services	10.6	10.0	9.6	11.0	10.0	7.9	9.5	11.1	10.0	8.7	7.8	7.4	7.3
Domestic services	5.8	..	5.0[g]	6.4[h]	5.0	..	2.3	..	..	..	..	2.8	2.5
Other personal services	4.8	..	4.6	4.6	5.0	..	7.2	..	..	..	..	4.6	4.8
C. Services without kibbutzim[i]	45.4	49.1	48.8	43.6	49.4	..	46.4	..	50.9	..	50.0	50.6	52.6
Kibbutzim	–	–	2.3	2.4	2.2	..	2.8	..	1.5	..	1.8	1.5	1.5
D. Total employed persons[j]	65.7	156.5	188.0	211.0	233.2	253	311.8	505	474.4	542.3	627.8	687.7	656.3

[a] 1931, 1948 and 1961 (2)—enumeration; 1954, 1955, 1959, 1961 (1)—sample surveys; for other years see Source.
[b] Includes income recipients other than employed persons. Most of these are concentrated in services, especially in commerce.
[c] Includes garage workers, classified in industry in subsequent years.   [e] The breakdown of this item is apparently not consistent with that used in other years.
[d] Electricity and national water supply in industry; municipal waterworks and sanitary services in general government.   [f] The figure apparently includes some items which should be in other public services.
[g] Includes some items which should be in other personal services.   [h] Includes public institutions' cleaning staffs.
[i] Per cent of total excluding kibbutzim.   [j] Thousands.

SOURCE: 1931, 1948 and 1961 (2)—Table 4.5
1936—Based on A. L. Gruenbaum (Gaathon) data.
1939, 1943, 1945—Based on Jewish Agency data.
1947, 1951—SBI Part A, July 1953, p. 193 (A. Nizan's data).
1954-61 (1)—Labour Force Surveys of the CBS:
1954—Special Series Nos. 25 and 56.
1955—SAI 1963, No. 14, p. 500.
1959, 1961 (1)—CBS, Labour Force Part I, op. cit.

TABLE 4.7   Jewish Employed Persons in Services: Selected Years

	1931 (per cent of total employed persons)	1931	1936	1945	1948	1954	1961 LFS	1961 Census
Total services in thousands		26.8	73.5	113.1	129.2	239.0	352.9	339.4
A. Per cent of total services								
Total services		100.0	100.0	100.0	100.0	100.0	100.0	100.0
Transportation and commerce		43.2	42.9	39.0	40.6	38.4	36.9	36.3
Transportation		12.1	10.9	10.0	12.9	13.0	12.9	12.5
Trade		28.5	28.6	26.2	24.8	22.5	19.6	18.6
Finance		2.6	3.4	2.8	2.9	2.9	4.4	5.2
Public services		33.4	36.7	41.1	39.5	42.1	48.6	49.9
General government		4.7	13.6	15.0	16.0	16.6	18.3	21.1
Other public services		28.7	23.1	26.1	23.5	25.5	30.3	28.8
Personal services		23.4	20.4	19.9	19.9	19.5	14.5	13.8
B. Share of services in total employed persons—index (1931=100)								
Total services	45.4	100	108	112	106	114	113	118
Total excluding personal services in kibbutzim	45.4	100	108	109	102	112	112	116
Transportation and commerce	19.6	100	107	101	100	101	97	99
Transportation	5.5	100	97	93	114	123	123	123
Trade	12.9	100	108	103	92	90	77	77
Finance	1.2	100	139	119	115	124	191	232
Public services	15.2	100	119	137	125	144	165	175
General government	2.1	100	316	358	363	406	443	528
Other public services	13.1	100	87	101	86	101	120	118
Personal services excluding kibbutzim	10.6	100	94	75	65	81	57	56

SOURCE: Data underlying Table 4.6.

the adjustment. If 1961 labour force survey figures are substituted
for the census data,[21] the change is still smaller. The low 1948
figure is explained by the fact that in war-time below normal employment in services is usual. [22] If this is taken into account together with
the 1936, 1939 and 1945 data, it appears that most of the change in the
per cent of persons employed in services occurred at the beginning of
the period, from 1931 to 1936 (see Tables 4.6 and 4.7, panels B and C).
If we also accept that the Nizan series overestimates the share of
services, we must conclude that since 1936 there have in fact been only
slight and unimportant changes in the share of services in employment,
and that in any event the change does not exceed 3 to 7 per cent over
the period.

In product also, there was not much difference between the 1936
and the 1961 levels. In the intervening years, however, the two series
moved differently. While the employment share of services was fairly
steady throughout, we saw that the product share fluctuated—a decline
from 1936 to 1945, and a rise thereafter, especially in the early years
of the State.

Taken separately, however, the services branches did not all maintain
a constant level.

Transportation: The share of persons employed in transportation rose
from 5.5 per cent in 1931 to 6.6 per cent in 1961, or by 23 per cent
(Table 4.8). Again, it is misleading to draw conclusions from the
three censuses alone, since the data for the intervening years show some
fluctuations. In particular, employment contracted during the second
world war, and Nizan's figures show a higher share for the first few
years of the State. This is perhaps what actually happened, but it is
also possible that the figures reflect changes in definition introduced by
the LFS—from 1955 on, garage workers are not included in transportation. The rise over the period in the share of transport employment is
similar to what was found for product originating in the branch. [23] The
same correspondence is found for transportation sub-branches. Table
4.8 shows that in employment also, the share of shipping and aviation
rose, both in total employment and in transportation, while the share
of inland transportation (again both in total and in the branch)
declined.

---

[21] See the discussion on p. 9, and note 3 on that page.
[22] Compare, for example, the 1943 estimate (Table 4.6).
[23] See p. 81 and Table 4.1.

TABLE 4.8   *Jewish Employed Persons in Transportation: Selected Years*

	1931	1945	1948	1961 Census
A. Employed persons in transportation—				
thousands	3.2	11.3	16.6	42.3
B. Per cent of total	**5.5**	**5.1**	**6.2**	**6.7**
Railways	0.5	0.2	0.2	0.3
Road transportation	4.1	3.8	3.9	3.2
Shipping and aviation	0.2	0.7	1.1	1.4
PTT	0.7	0.4	0.9	0.9
Other transportation	..	..	0.1	0.9
C. Per cent of persons employed				
in transportation	**100.0**	**100.0**	**100.0**	**100.0**
Railways	8.4	4.9	3.6	4.6
Road transport	75.6	74.9	63.3	46.9
Shipping and aviation	3.5	13.2	17.0	21.4
PTT	12.5	7.0	14.0	13.7
Other transportation	..	..	2.1	13.4
D. Share of transportation in total employed persons—index (1931=100)				
Total transportation	100	93	114	123
Railways	100	54	48	67
Road transportation	100	92	94	76
Shipping and aviation	100	353	533	747
PTT	100	53	126	134

SOURCE: Data underlying Table 4.6.

Commerce: The share of trade in employment declined from 13 per cent in 1931 to 10 per cent in 1961. During the mandatory period, the level stayed at around 13 per cent, except during the second world war, when it declined. Since the establishment of the State, there is a clear downward trend from 1955 to 1961. [24]

Analysis of the Nizan figures shows that there was apparently no rise in the share of trade during 1948–55, especially at the time of

[24] According to the LFS the employment share of commerce (trade and finance) dropped from 14 to 12.3 per cent during this period, and all the evidence shows that the share of finance has been rising.

TABLE 4.9   *Jewish Employed Persons in Public Services:*
Selected Years

	1931	1945	1948	1961	
				LFS	Census
A. Total public services—thousands	8.9	46.4	51.1	171.5	169.5
B. Per cent of total employed persons					
All public services	**15.2**	**20.8**	**18.9**	**25.0**	**26.6**
General government	*2.1*	*7.6*	*7.7*	*9.4*	*11.2*
Central government[a]	1.6	4.7[c]	3.9	6.0	6.8
Local authorities	0.4	1.3	1.9	1.9	2.6
National institutions etc.	0.1	1.6	1.9	1.5	1.8
Other public services	*13.1*	*13.2*	*11.2*	*15.6*	*15.4*
Education[b]	5.8	4.6	4.7	7.5	7.2
Health	3.1	2.8	3.9	4.7	4.4
Welfare	0.1	0.1	0.5	0.9	0.9
Religious institutions	1.3	0.6	0.5	0.3	0.2
Other community services	2.8	5.1[d]	1.6	2.2	2.7
C. Share of public services in total: Index (1931=100)					
All public services	100	137	125	165	176
General government	100	356	361	443	532
Central government[a]	100	289	242	375	422
Other general government	100	569	739	659	876
Other public services	100	101	86	119	118
Education[b]	100	79	81	130	124
Health	100	92	129	152	143
Religious services	100	47	42	22	18
Other community services	100	180	72	106	123
[a] Of which: Police—					
per cent	0.8	2.2	0.9	1.1	1.1
index, 1931=100	100	267	111	131	137
[b] Education excluding yeshivot—					
per cent	4.3	3.7	..	..	6.7
index, 1931 = 100	100	85	..	..	155

[c] Includes 2,200 civilian War Department employees.
[d] Includes about 4,500 cleaning staff of various institutions.
SOURCE: Data underlying Table 4.6.

mass immigration. The share of trade stood at 12–13 per cent in these years, and began to decline only thereafter. Comparison with the product figures,[25] indicates that since the establishment of the State the two magnitudes have been moving in the same direction and very roughly at the same rate; during the mandatory period, however, there was a steep decline in the product share of trade, while the employment share did not change.

The employment share of finance almost doubled according to the LFS data, and rose by much more according to the Census. During the mandatory period there was only a small net increase in the branch, apparently the result of expansion in the mid-thirties and contraction during the war years. Most of the expansion in this branch occurred in the period of the State, when the rise in employment was accompanied by a rise in the product share. At least some of the decline in the product share which occurred during the mandatory period was contemporaneous (1939–45) with the decline in the share of employment, as far as can be seen from the available data.

Public services: The employment share of this group of service branches rose from 15.2 per cent in 1931 to 25.0 per cent in 1961 (according to LFS; more, according to the Census). The increase was continuous throughout the period, but was rather more rapid in the 1930's and in the 1950's. Table 4.9 shows the figures for the branches of the group.

The share of general government rose from 2.1 to 9.4 per cent (11.2 per cent according to the Census), or at least four and a half times. This increase reflects a rise in the share of each of the components. [26] As far as may be judged, the increase was continuous, and occurred also during the mandatory period; in fact, most of the rise in the share of local authorities and national institutions had occurred by 1948. In central government, the employment share rose from 1.6 to 3.9 per cent over 1931–48 and only to 6–6.8 per cent thereafter. [27] Subdividing the period at 1945 does not much affect the picture. If police (and the civilian employees of the British War Department in 1945) [28] are excluded from other civil servants the results are somewhat different: the share of the civil service rose from about 1 per cent in 1931 to about 1.5 per cent in 1945 and 3 per cent in 1948, and later to 5 or 6

25 See pp. 82–83 and Table 4.1.
26 Central government, local authorities, and national institutions etc.
27 The Nizan figures apparently used a different classification for the distinction between general government and public services, so that the same total is not broken down as in the rest of the period.
28 The figures in note a of Table 4.9 refer only to police.

per cent in 1961. In other words, most of the increase in central government administrative services did in fact occur with the establishment of the State. Nevertheless, police and supernumeraries were an important element in the rise of Jewish employment in the government sector during the period surveyed. With the establishment of the State, the share of police in Jewish employment dropped from the 1945 level.

In 'other public services' the picture is somewhat different, principally because the rise in the employment share was much more moderate than in general government. In effect, the increase occurred from 1954 on. There may have been a temporary decline at the end of the 1940's. The marked change seen in the 1943 estimate may be partly due to changes in the classification of general government services and partly to the fact that many professional persons were called up or joined the British army as civilian employees.

Within 'other public services' (Table 4.9) the shares of religious services and yeshivot (religious colleges) [29] declined; the share of educational services rose—after an initial decline—mainly after the establishment of the State. This increase by itself explains over half of the rise in the share of the whole branch. There was a more moderate rise in the share of health services, and the share of welfare services also rose. There is no separate information for other sub-branches in the group.

We saw in the case of product that the share of public services rose mostly with the establishment of the State, and declined slightly in the second half of the State period, during which the employment share continued to rise. [30]

The principal conclusion to be drawn from the data is that although the establishment of the State and the consequent demographic changes were reflected in an increase in the employment share of public services, there was no marked jump; in fact, during the two decades preceding the establishment of the State a growing proportion of employed persons was absorbed by public services—mainly in general government. The supply by the Jewish sector of general government services, and of community services such as health and education preceded the establishment of the State, and advanced with the growth of the sector, and its economic consolidation.

Personal services: Scanty and unreliable information does not permit us to say much about this group. According to available data (Tables 4.5 and 4.6), the employment share of personal services declined from

[29] See note b in Table 4.9.
[30] See pp. 83–84 and Table 4.1.

10.6 per cent at the beginning of the period to 7.4 per cent at the end; this rather steep drop occurred despite the fact that in 1931 personal services in kibbutzim were not included. [31] Most of the decline reflects the drop in domestic service, from about 6 per cent during the Mandate to about 2 per cent in 1961 (excluding kibbutzim). There are no marked changes in the share of the other sub-branches. The product share of personal services declined less steeply than their employment share. [32]

Other branches: The chief changes in other branches were as follows: the share of agriculture in employment dropped from about 20 per cent in the 1930's to 13–14 per cent after the second world war, and there have been only slight changes since. [33] In industry (which here includes also power generation and part of waterworks) the principal changes were due to the second world war—as we saw this was also true of product. As a result of the war there was a steep rise in the employment share of the branch during the war years, followed by a decline in the post-war period, which apparently continued through the early years of the State. From the low point in 1951 the employment share of industry rose slowly and steadily until 1961. The share of construction was fairly constant in the long run, and usually fluctuated round 8–9 per cent.

The combined effect of these changes altered the within-services composition considerably, as may be seen in Table 4.7, panel A. On the one hand, the share of trade dropped from 28 to 20 per cent, [34] and that of personal services from 23 to 14 per cent; on the other hand, general government rose steeply from about 5 per cent to at least 18 per cent, and finance also rose considerably from 2.6 per cent to 4–5 per cent. The shares of transportation (about 12.5 per cent) and 'other public services' (about 30 per cent) were the same at each end of the period, although the share of 'other public services' declined from 1936 to 1954.

The product-worker ratio

The statistical and conceptual problems of this series have already been discussed in the introduction and on p. 15. The figures for the period of the State were calculated from the total (Jews and non-Jews)

---

[31] See panel C of Table 4.6 and p. 86. Excluding kibbutzim, the 1961 figure would be 6 per cent.

[32] See p. 84 and Table 4.1.

[33] However, see p. 9 for a discussion of the Census results.

[34] Here and in the rest of this paragraph, figures are in per cent of persons employed in 'all services'.

TABLE 4.10   *The Product-Worker Ratio: Selected Years*[a]

	1936	1945[b]	1951	1954	1955	1959	1961 LFS	1961 Census

A. Product-worker ratio[c]

1. Total	1.00	1.00	1.00	1.00	1.00	1.00	1.00	1.00
Agriculture	0.52	0.79	0.44	0.73	0.71	0.81	0.70	0.86
Industry	1.29	1.30	1.06	1.13	1.18	1.10	1.15	1.11
Construction	1.13	0.97	1.09	0.92	0.96	0.86	0.88	0.92
Public utilities[d]	..	..	..	1.08	0.89	0.98	1.28	1.10
Services	1.07	0.87	1.14	1.05	1.04	1.05	1.04	0.99
2. Services	1.07	0.87	1.14[e]	1.05	1.04	1.05	1.04	0.99
Transportation	1.41	1.34	1.50	1.22	1.23	1.24	1.27	1.25
Commerce	1.86	1.27	1.06	1.22	1.16	1.31	1.38	1.34
Trade	1.68	..	..	1.14	1.10	1.24	1.29	1.29
Finance	3.35	..	..	1.84	1.56	1.65	1.80	1.51
Public and personal services	0.56	0.58	1.12[f]	0.94	0.94	0.90	0.86	0.81
Public services	..	..	..	1.06	0.99	0.93	0.87	0.80
Personal services	..	..	..	0.70	0.80	0.80	0.83	0.83

B. Product-worker ratio in services—index[g] (1936=100)

2. Total services	100	81	107	98	97	98	97	93
Transportation	100	95	106	87	87	88	90	89
Commerce	100	68	57	66	62	70	74	72
Trade	100	..	..	68	65	74	77	77
Finance	100	..	..	55	47	49	54	45
Personal and public services	100	104	200	168	168	161	154	145

[a] 1936 and 1945—Jewish sector of Palestine only. For 1951, the source employment figures were for Jews only, and have here been adjusted to include non-Jews.
[b] 5,000 employed in kibbutz services have been excluded since they are apparently not covered by income figures.
[c] 1961 has NDP variant II (see note c to Table 4.1).
[d] The product of municipal sanitation services is included in general government, so that the ratio is understated. If the 1961 Census labour force figures are adjusted for this, the ratio is 1.67 instead of 1.10.
[e] PTT is included in general government and not in transportation.
[f] Product includes a partial estimate of ownership of dwellings.
[g] Calculated from panel A.
SOURCE: Labour force—see Table 4.6 sources.
          Net product—see Table 4.1 sources; the figures have here been adjusted to fit the employment data.

employed labour force, in order to make them consistent with the product figures. Similarly, wherever possible, the adjustments listed on p. 13 have been made to the product figures.

Table 4.10 shows the product-worker ratio of the various branches over the period. For the mandatory period there are only two observations (as for the product series)—1936 and 1945. From 1954 on there are, as stated, continuous series for both NDP and employed labour force. [35]

The salient feature of the product-worker ratio for all services together is the similarity of the two end-years of the period. Clearly, this is consistent with the development of product and employment from 1936 to 1961. In the sub-periods there was a decline in the ratio from 1936 to 1945, while the ratio was more or less steady in the period 1954–61 at a higher level than in 1945. The conclusion is that there was an increase in the ratio at some time between 1945 and 1954. [36]

The ratio for 'all services' is slightly above the average for the economy. As we have seen, this may be an underestimate.

Transportation: Throughout the period the product-worker ratio in this branch is considerably above the average, although it declined from 1.41 in 1936 to 1.27 in 1961.

Commerce: In trade the ratio is also above the average for the economy throughout the period, and lower in 1961 than in 1936. The steepest drop occurred in 1936–45, [37] and may have continued until the early years of the State. [38] From 1954 or 1955 until 1961 there is some tendency for the ratio to rise.

Throughout the period, finance has the highest product-worker ratio although the decline from beginning to end of the period was considerable. As with trade, most of the decline apparently occurred between 1936 and 1945. Since 1954 the ratio has fluctuated strongly. It reached its lowest level in 1954–58, and in recent years (1958–1961) it has again risen.

For distributive services and finance together, there was a net decline in the product-worker ratio from 1936 to 1961. At the same time, the commerce ratio has tended to rise in recent years. The distributive

[35] However, a more or less complete adjustment between product and employment figures was made only for 1961 and used only in Table 2.4. See Section 1 of Chapter 2.

[36] According to the 1951 data, this increase took place only from 1951 to 1954, but as stated, the 1951 figures are open to doubt.

[37] This can easily be seen from the figure of 1.27 for commerce.

[38] On the basis of either the 1951 or the 1954–55 figures.

services and finance group have the highest product-worker ratio of all branches.

Public and personal services: For the transition from Mandate to State the product-worker ratio is in Table 4.10 shown only for the group as a whole, owing to the impossibility of reconciling the product and labour force classifications. In the second sub-period, the ratio was much higher than in the first, while it was fairly steady during each period; throughout, the ratio was below the national average. Because of the importance of general government and other public services in the group it is clear that the marked change in the ratio must be due to these branches. Crude separate figures for general government and 'other public services' in 1945 show that the ratio was lower in 'other public services'. [39] Comparison with the 1961 figures suggests that the principal increase in the product-worker ratio occurred in 'other public services', while in general government the changes were more moderate. The rather low level of the 'other public services' ratio will be discussed later, and we shall attempt to decide to what extent this low level (which exists, whether or not our speculations are sound) was due to the relatively large supply of professional persons. Part of the increase in the product-worker ratio of general government and public services is clearly due to the change in the composition of general government employment, i.e., the shift of emphasis from police to civil servants. The increase in wage differentials over the period may also be a contributory cause.

The unadjusted figures show a rise in the ratio for personal services —which was to be expected in view of the decline in the weight of domestic services (which have the lowest product-worker ratio).

In the non-service branches we find a very low product-worker ratio for agriculture (but the high weight of the Arab sector in this branch for the figures from 1951 on should be borne in mind); in construction the ratio is lower than the national average, at least in recent years, and in manufacturing it is higher. [40]

Summarizing our meagre information on the product-worker ratio for services from 1936 to 1961, we see a fairly constant level—close to

[39] The ratio obtained for general government is 0.77 while for public services we get a *maximum* of 0.45 (based on calculations from the employment and product tables after the relevant adjustments). For personal services the same calculation gives a maximum of 0.67 and a minimum of 0.53.

[40] There is apparently some overestimate here, resulting from a combination of minor factors, such as the absence of a depreciation or stock-valuation adjustment.

TABLE 4.11   Summary of the Principal Changes During the Period[a]

	1936–61	Pre-State period		Transition	State
		1931–36	from 1936		
All services					
Product share	1		−1	2	0
Employment share	1	2	(0)	1	0
Product-worker ratio	−1	(0)	−2	2	0
Transportation					
Product share	1	0	0	1	1
Employment share	2	0	0	2	0
Product-worker ratio	−1	−1	−1	0	0
Trade					
Product share	−3	(−2)	(−2)	(−1)	−1
Employment share	−2	−1	−1	0	−1
Product-worker ratio	−2	1	−1	(0)	1
Finance					
Product share	−2	(−2)	−1	..	1
Employment share	1	1	1	(1)	1
Product-worker ratio	−3	−1	−3	(0)	1
Public services					
Product share	3	2	2	2	0
Employment share	2	1	2	(1)	1
Product-worker ratio	(2)	1	(2)	(2)	−1
General government					
Product share	(2)	(1)	(1)	1	..
Employment share	2	1	1	0	1
Product-worker ratio	(1)	..	..	(1)	..
Other public services					
Product share	2	..	(0)	2	2
Employment share	1	−1	1	1	1
Product-worker ratio	(2)	..	..	..	2
Personal services					
Product share	1	1	1	1	−1
Employment share	1	−1	1	0	−1
Product-worker ratio	(2)	−1	(0)	(1)	1

[a] The limits of the sub-periods vary according to the data available.
Numbers indicate three degrees of increase or decrease (−), in ascending order of intensity.
SOURCE: Tables 4.1, 4.6, and 4.10.

the national average. Over the period, the ratio for distributive services
and finance, and that for public and personal services, have both converged towards the national average; in the first group, the ratio is
still well above average, and in the second it is fairly close to average.
In some branches (trade, finance, and perhaps public services) the
trend was reversed in recent years.

Summary

Table 4.11 gives a qualitative summary of the changes which occurred
in the share of services between 1931 (1936) and 1961, for three sub-
periods: that part of the mandatory period covered by the study, a
transitional period covering the latter years of the Mandate and the
early years of the State, and the period of the State. (The actual
limits of the three sub-periods vary according to the indicator under
consideration.) From this table, and from the tables on which it is
based, the following points emerge:

a.   There were only small (upward) changes in the weight of services
in the economy, whether measured in terms of product or of employment. At the same time the product-worker ratio declined slightly.
These slight net changes consisted of a decline in the product share
and in the product-worker ratio in the first part of the period, and a
rise after the establishment of the State. The 'all services' figures mask
much greater internal changes.

b.   Over the period the employment and product shares of trade
declined. During the Mandate the product share dropped further so that
the product-worker ratio declined. Although the weight of the branch
continued to decline up to 1961, there are signs in recent years of a
rise in the product-worker ratio.

c.   The expanding branches in the distributive services and finance
group are:

i.   Transportation, which increased its share in both employment
and product, while the product-worker ratio declined somewhat in the
first part of the period. The increase was in shipping and aviation and
not in inland transportation.

ii.   Throughout the period finance has expanded in terms of the
employment share, while the product share declined considerably during
the first period, and rose thereafter; the product-worker ratio also
declined greatly in the first period (and, according to the LFS figures in
the second period).

d.   According to all three criteria public services expanded in all
sub-branches except police and religious services.

General government began at a very low level, and rose continuously throughout the period, and—as far as the figures show—not abruptly when the State was established: this is especially true of the employment share. After the establishment of the State the product share rose more rapidly than the employment share, so that the product-worker ratio rose.

Most of the expansion in 'other public services'—whether in terms of employment or of product—occurred after the establishment of the State; this was to a great extent due to the relatively high level (at least in employment terms) of these services during the mandatory period. After the establishment of the State there was also a steep rise in the product-worker ratio.

   e.   Personal services can be described as a contracting branch because of the decline in domestic services, which outweighed the slight expansion of the other sub-branches. For the branch, the employment and product shares declined, and the product-worker ratio rose from the mandatory to the State period.

   f.   Together, these developments brought about a radical change in the internal structure of services. To put it in the most general terms, the centre of gravity is passing from commerce, and to some extent personal services, to general government and, to some extent, the other public services.

2.   INTERNATIONAL COMPARISON—THE TIME SERIES

As pointed out in Chapter 2 (Section 2), the countries cross-section and the time series for single countries gave similar pictures of industrial structure. This broad similarity shows that economic growth is the principal factor governing structural changes. It is not, however, surprising that the results of each type of study differ somewhat in both degree and kind. Historical trends as well as specific events are at work over the years, in addition to factors discernible at a point in time. Worldwide technological improvements, changes in international communications, and changes in the values, aims, and tastes of individuals, societies, and governments, are examples of general historical movements.

The principal findings of the cross-section have already been discussed in Chapter 2. Compared with the cross-section, our historical information is meagre, and any conclusions are necessarily tentative.[41]

[41] This section deals with the Jewish sector only. Since our discussion is

All services

The employment share of services rose more slowly in Israel than in other countries during periods of similar length, especially if we take 1936–61 for Israel: during thirty-one of forty 30–35 year periods within the last hundred years (in about 30 countries) the employment share of services rose by more than 5 percentage points, declining in only two of the periods. [42] In Israel (Table 4.6) the share rose by 6 to 8 points from 1931 to 1961, and by only 2 to 4 percentage points from 1936 to 1961. [43] The indexes based on the first year of our series show even more clearly that the change has been comparatively slight in Israel. This finding is the more remarkable when viewed against the dynamic development of the Jewish sector, reflected in the rapid growth of product and labour force. In his international study Kuznets showed that there was a connexion between the rate of structural change (in terms of employment) and the rate of growth, [44] but the services sector was not considered separately. In the Kuznets study of the American states, services (and some of the sub-branches) were examined separately. His principal finding is that in most cases there is a positive correlation between the rate of growth of per capita product, and long-run changes in the share of services (both in product and employment). [45] The Jewish sector of Palestine had one of the highest rates of growth of per capita product in the world, [46] so that dynamic changes in the employment share of services might have been expected. It is not necessary to bring evidence that during our period employed labour force

---

qualitative on the whole, it does not matter much that the product figures for the period of the State are for the whole population.

[42] In 17 periods the share increased by more than 10 percentage points. See S. Kuznets, *Countries,* pp. 28–31, Table 14.

[43] The lower figure uses the LFS data, and as stated, seems to be more reliable for large branches. All data exclude personal services in kibbutzim. (See Table 4.6).

[44] S. Kuznets, *Countries,* pp. 52–55.

[45] S. Kuznets, *States,* p. 39, and *passim.*

[46] The per capita national income of the Jewish sector of Palestine rose by 25 per cent from 1936 to 1947, and by about 5 per cent annually from 1950 to 1962, or 60 per cent over the decade. These rates may be compared with those for other countries in S. Kuznets, "Quantitative Aspects of the Economic Growth of Nations, I. Levels and Variability of Rates of Growth," *Economic Development and Cultural Change,* Vol. V, No. 1, October 1956, pp. 10–15, Tables 1 to 3.

grew more rapidly in Israel than in all other periods and countries available for comparison; there is also no doubt that such dynamic changes can affect economic structure.

The data on the product share of services do not permit any generalization: the indicator rises in some and declines in other countries, and in about half the periods the changes are less than 5 percentage points. [47] In the period reviewed, the product share of services in Israel declined by about 3 percentage points from 58 per cent. [48] This is not particularly remarkable when compared with the international findings. The (slight) decline in product share fits another generalization stated by Kuznets *(loc. cit.)* on the basis of his findings: that a decline in the product share of services occurs in countries where the initial share was high.

The international data (and those for the states of the US) show a steep decline in the product-worker ratio of services. As with employment shares, the changes were more marked in the time series than in the cross-section. The ratios decline in 12 of the 15 periods for which the calculation was made, in most of them by 50 per cent or more; in the other three it rose. In every case the ratio converged towards the average (i.e., unity). [49] In Israel the ratio declined slightly from about 1.19 to 1.11, [50] but the decline is much smaller than that found in any of the other countries where the ratio declined; in this sense, Israel is exceptional. At the same time, the initial level of the ratio was considerably lower in Israel than in the other countries where there was a decline.

At the beginning of the period, and throughout, the volume of services in Israel was above the international norm. This is clear from the fact that the services share was roughly the same at both ends of the period, and that per capita income rose considerably. Overconcentration of employment (and product) in services was thus much more serious at the beginning of the period than at its end. [51] The phenomenon was in fact recognized at the time by many students of the country's

---

[47] S. Kuznets, *Countries*, pp. 18–19, Table 7.
[48] Includes ownership of dwellings, for the sake of consistency with the international data.
[49] S. Kuznets, *Countries*, pp. 48–49.
[50] The 1936 figure is calculated from a product share of 58.3 per cent (Table 4.1) and an employment share of 49.1 per cent (Table 4.6). The 1961 figure is taken from Table 2.6 and covers the whole population.
[51] See Table 4.12 for a crude calculation.

TABLE 4.12   *The Employment Share of Services* *in Palestine
and other Countries*

(per cent)

	Jewish sector of Palestine 1936	*Country-group IV average* [b]	*Regression (for $ 250 per capita* [c]*)*
S	49.1	23.7	27.6
T+C	21.0	9.4	11.8
T	5.3	3.3	4.0
C	14.0	6.1	7.8
OS	28.1	14.2	16.5

[a] Symbols for subsectors are explained in Table 2.6.
[b] The average per capita income of this group is $ 270.
[c] National income for the Jewish sector of Palestine is based on Gaathon's
   estimates (in *Encyclopaedia Hebraica,* Vol. VI, p. 730, Table 2 and p. 738,
   Table 9).
   The calculation is necessarily crude, and the unreliability of the result should
   be stressed.
SOURCE: Column (1)—Table 4.6.
       Column (2)—Table 2.5, Panel B.
       Column (3)—Calculated from the Kuznets *Countries* data.

industrial structure. [52] It may well be that the share of services changed
so little over the period because of the initially high overconcentration.

The services sub-branches

The employment share of transportation in Israel rose over the period.
This is consistent with both the cross-section findings and the historical
development in most of the countries for which we have data. However, in many countries the share of this branch has recently declined
after a long period of increase; this seems to be partly due to recent
rapid technological changes; there is also a tendency for some transport
services to be supplied by households instead of by enterprises, as the
use of private vehicles spreads. [53] The decline is not yet felt in Israel,

[52] See for example, L. Gruenbaum (Gaathon), *National Income and Outlay in
   Palestine 1936,* Jerusalem, 1941, p. 26, and *Outlines for a Development Plan
   for Palestine,* Jewish Agency, 1946, pp. 85, 98, 101–102.
[53] The share of transportation rose until recently in all 16 countries for which
   we have information; in eight of them, the rise was arrested or reversed in
   recent years. See S. Kuznets, *Countries,* pp. 82–95, Appendix Table 4. Much
   of the data shown there is taken from Colin Clark, *The Conditions of Economic Progress* (third edition), London, 1957. Most of the countries included
   are developed, and it may be assumed that in the less developed ones the

probably because shipping and aviation continue to expand, and because the shift of inland passenger transportation to households is not as far advanced as in the most developed countries. Historical information on the product share of transportation is available for only a few countries; in most of these the share tends to decline, in contrast to the (moderate) rise found in Israel. [54] It should be remembered that the cross-section showed a tendency for the product share of transportation to rise. In Israel, the product-worker ratio declined slightly in the first part of the period and was stable thereafter; this is broadly consistent with the findings for the American states. [55] In general it may be said that the moderate rate at which transportation expanded throughout the period in Israel was somewhat more rapid than that found in other countries in recent years, although fairly similar to that found at earlier stages of development.

All existing studies show a steep rise in the employment share of commerce, unlike in Israel, where there was a drop from 14.2 per cent in 1931 and 15 per cent in 1936, to about 12.5 per cent in 1961. In most countries in which the employment share of services rose, the increase is due mainly to transportation and commerce (the T+C sector in the Kuznets classification). The available data on transportation show that most of the rise is concentrated in commerce. [56] There are no data for the trade and finance components of this sector separately, but the small weight of finance suggests that most of the rise is concentrated in trade. This is confirmed by Stigler's study on the United States. [57] Israel differs from the other countries chiefly in trade, since the employment share of finance rose markedly over the period. This further highlights the decline in the employment share of trade from 13–14 per cent at the beginning of the period to about 10 per cent at its end. The product share of commerce declined sharply in Israel throughout the period, and it is only in recent years that a reversal of the trend has appeared in finance. The product share of commerce declined in some countries but rose in others. [58] The product-worker ratio of commerce declined in Israel, and this was also found in the

---

employment share of transportation continues to rise.

[54] S. Kuznets, *Countries*, pp. 68–74, Appendix Table 2.

[55] S. Kuznets, *States*, p. 79, Table 33.

[56] S. Kuznets, *Countries*, pp. 28–31, Table 14, and pp. 82–95, Appendix Table 14.

[57] G.J. Stigler, *Trends in Employment in the Service Industries*, NBER, Princeton, 1956, p. 7, Table 4.

[58] S. Kuznets, *Countries*, pp. 68–74, Appendix Table 2.

American States. [59] It is the recent rise in the ratio for trade that is somewhat out of line with the other countries.

Since trade is the most important component of the $T+C$ sector, the latter's employment share declines despite the rise in the share of finance and transportation; except for Yugoslavia, Israel is the only country for which we have information where this is so.

In most countries, including Israel, the employment share of the OS sector has risen in the course of time. In Israel, however, the change is more marked, and is matched in only a few other countries. The OS sector in Israel is in fact 'responsible' for the rise in the employment share of 'all services.' [60] The data are not adequate for a sound comparison of the product share and the product-worker ratio in this sector. However, fragmentary data suggest that the steep increase which occurred in Israel is exceptional—in extent, if not in direction. [61]

In contrast to the cross-section, the time series shows a marked rise in the employment and product shares of general government. [62] This is due to the change in the conventional idea of the role of government which has taken place during the last hundred years. In Israel we find an increase in the employment share over the period, somewhat steeper than in other countries. This is undoubtedly due to the change of regime (1948). The rise in the product worker ratio seems to have no parallel in other countries.

The rise in the employment share of 'other public services' (liberal professions) is common to Israel and other countries. A comparison with the US for a roughly corresponding period shows that the rate of

---

[59] S. Kuznets, *States*, p. 51, Table 19.

[60] S. Kuznets, *Countries*, pp. 28–31, Table 14.

[61] *Ibid.*, Appendix Table 1; as can be seen from this source the time series show changes in both directions for product share, while in the US the product-worker ratio declined despite the rise in product share (S. Kuznets, *States*, p. 79, Table 33).

[62] Oshima found that the share of government budgets in national income was higher after the second world war than before. (H.T. Oshima, "Share of Government in Gross National Product for Various Countries," *The American Economic Review*, June 1957).

Data on the employment share of government in the UK and the US, and detailed discussion of why the share has risen are found in S. Fabricant, *Trends in Government Activity Since 1900*, NBER, New York, 1952, and M. Abramovitz and V.F. Eliasberg, *The Growth of Public Employment in Great Britain*, NBER, Princeton, 1957.

TABLE 4.13   *The Employment Share of Selected Services:*
Palestine and the United States[a]

(per cent)

	United States 1930	Jewish sector of Palestine	
		1931	1945
Trade	13.1	12.9	13.3
Finance	3.1	1.2	1.4
General government	2.4	2.1	7.6[b]
Other public services	7.1[c]	13.1	13.2[d]
of which: Education	3.4	5.8 (4.3)[e]	4.6
Domestic services	5.4	5.8	5.0
Other personal services	5.3	4.8	5.0

[a] Per capita national income (at 1954 prices): US, 1930—about $ 960.
   Palestine (Jewish sector), 1936—about $ 250; 1945—about $ 310.
[b] Includes watchmen, supernumerary police, and British Army clerks (about
   3 per cent in all).
[c] Includes recreation (about 1 per cent).
[d] Includes cleaners in public institutions (about 2 per cent).
[e] The figure in parenthesis does not include yeshivot.
SOURCE: United States—G. J. Stigler, *Trends in Employment in the Service*
   Industries, NBER, Princeton, 1957, p. 7 Table 4, and p. 24.
   Palestine—Tables 4.5 and 4.6.

increase was much higher in the US than in Israel. [63] A decline in the
product-worker ratio of this branch recurs constantly in different countries, both in cross-section and time-series studies. Israel's persistently
rising ratio is therefore exceptional.

The decline in the employment share of domestic services is consistent
with the cross-section and some time-series findings. This is true also of
the tendency for the share of several small personal services sub-branches
to rise (e.g., recreation). However, cleaning services and restaurants
contracted somewhat in Israel, unlike in other countries. [64]

The points of employment overconcentration shifted radically from
the beginning to the end of the period. Some differences can be listed
even without attempting precise calculations (see Tables 4.6 and 4.7).

At the beginning of the period, there was considerable overconcentration in trade: during the Mandate the employment share of this branch

[63] In this comparison, 1920–50 was taken for the US. The conclusion is not
   valid for education unless a slightly longer period is taken for the US.
   See G.J. Stigler, *loc. cit.*
[64] *Ibid.,* Chapter 5, and S. Kuznets, *States.*

was 3 or 4 percentage points higher than in 1961; had Israel's development been similar to that of other countries it should have been lower to this extent. (Compare the US data for 1930 in Table 4.13.)

There was overconcentration in personal services at the beginning of the period.

There was no overconcentration in general government at the beginning of the period. The volume of these services was almost certainly below normal in 1931, and perhaps also in 1936.

The only feature common to both ends of the period is the employment overconcentration in 'other public services,' but here too, it was more acute at the beginning than at the end of the period. Table 4.13 shows that during the mandatory period the employment share of this branch was almost double what it was in the US at the same time. The product-worker ratio was much lower at the beginning than at the end of the period—again in contrast to world trends—and this also points to a more acute overconcentration in the early period. Tables 4.12 and 4.13 provide a crude illustration of the extent and location of services overconcentration.

Chapter 5: The Times Series: Analysis

In this chapter we try to explain the findings of Chapter 4, and we discuss how far the time series supports the analysis of Chapter 3; in other words, whether the explanations of overconcentration found for 1961 also fit the facts of the whole period. We shall also examine in greater detail the effect on services of disguised unemployment.

1. THE FOREIGN TRADE EFFECTS

As stated, the internal composition of services was different at the two ends of the period, and there was more overconcentration at the beginning and during the period than at its end. We can thus examine the various arguments of Chapter 3 about the factors currently affecting economic structure. The marked changes found also raise the question of whether there are any factors which operated at one time or another, and which are inactive or difficult to detect at a point in time. We shall here deal with points considered in detail for the cross-section, and we shall extend the discussion of disguised unemployment and the occupational structure of immigrants.

In the 1961 discussion, our principal conclusions about the effect of the import surplus on industrial structure were as follows:

   a.   The income effect accounts for only a small part of services overconcentration.

   b.   The substitution effect is considerable, and can explain most of the overconcentration.

   c.   The income and substitution effects are at work chiefly in public services, and to a small extent in trade and transportation.

The three factors which determine the extent of the import surplus effect are, therefore, (1) the relative size of the import surplus; (2) its industrial composition; and (3) the allocation of capital imports.

Tables 5.1 and 5.2 present crude global data on these three aspects of the import surplus. From this and other information the following conclusions may be drawn:

   a.   Throughout (except during the second world war), the import surplus declined as a percentage of net product (Table 5.1). At current prices [1] and at the official exchange rates, it declined from 40 per

---

[1] The use of current prices is appropriate in our context, since it is our purpose

TABLE 5.1   *The Import Surplus in Israel: Selected Years*

Import surplus as per cent of national income[a]			Composition of import surplus			
Year	A (1)	B (2)	Period	Total (3)	Goods (4)	Services (5)
			1932–35	100	102	−2
			1936–39	100	101	−1
1936	40		1936 (Jews)	100	96	4
			1936 (non-Jews)	100	87	13
1939	44					
			1940–45	−100[b]	150	−250
			1946	100	225	−125
1950	30	..				
1952	33	35	1949–54[c]	100	90(95)	10(5)
1954	27	30				
1955	31	36				
1958	23	29	1955–61[c]	100	82(96)	18(4)
1961	18	25				

[a] A—at the official exchange rates; B—at effective exchange rates (i.e. including import taxes net of export subsidies).
[b] Export surplus.
[c] Government n.e.s. is included in services. The figures in parentheses show a crude adjustment made by transferring 80 per cent of the items to goods.
SOURCE: Columns (1) and (2):
A. L. Gaathon, in *Encyclopaedia Hebraica*, Vol. VI, pp. 729–30 (for national income in 1936 and 1939).
L. Gruenbaum (Gaathon), *National Income and Outlay in Palestine 1936*, Jerusalem, 1941, pp. 92–93 (for 1936 import surplus).
Jewish Agency, *Statistical Handbook of Jewish Palestine 1947*, Jerusalem, p. 375 (for 1939 import surplus).
NAD, *Israel's National Income and Expenditure (1950–1962)*, CBS Special Series No. 153, 1964 (for all 1950–61 figures).
Columns (3) to (5):
A. Kessler, in *Encyclopaedia Hebraica*, Vol. VI, pp. 749–50 (for Palestine) and pp. 751–52 (for Israel, 1949–54).
L. Gruenbaum (Gaathon), *op. cit.*, pp. 92–93 (for Jews and non-Jews, 1936).
Bank of Israel, *Annual Reports*, various issues (for 1955–61).

TABLE 5.2   *Capital Imports, by Recipient—Jewish Sector*

(per cent)

	Total	Public	Private
1917/18–1944/45	100	29	71
1931/32–1938/39	100	15	85
1939/40–1944/45	100	49	51
1949–1959	100	75	25

SOURCE: Jewish Agency, *Statistical Handbook of Jewish Palestine 1947*, p. 375 and M. Michaely, *Foreign Trade and Capital Import in Israel*, Am Oved, 1963, p. 36.

cent of product in the 1930's to 30 per cent in the early years of the State, and to 20 per cent in the later years. We have noted that services overconcentration is more marked at the beginning of the period than in 1961. Since import surplus effects are of great importance, the decline in the surplus in itself contributed to the lessening of overconcentration.

b.   Table 5.1 also shows the import surplus broken down into goods and services; scarcely any adjustment has been made. The salient finding of the table is that throughout the period (again, except for the war) there were no marked changes in composition. Gaathon's 1936 figures give the same result as the data for the period of the State adjusted for government services (largely defence imports). However, the balance of payments of the Jewish sector may well have been abnormal in 1936; estimates for the whole country (several years taken together) show a net export of services, and we may therefore conclude that in the 1930's the Jewish sector had some surplus of services exports (about 3 to 5 per cent of the import surplus); this means that the share of services in the import surplus is higher in recent years than in the 1930's. If this is so, then the more acute overconcentration of the 1930's (as compared with the years since 1948) is in part also due to the composition of the import surplus: during the State period this has not changed, so that its effects should also not have varied.

c.   Only 30 per cent of Jewish sector capital imports reached the public and national institutions during the mandatory period (only 15 per cent in the 1930's). After 1948 the proportions were almost reversed (see Table 5.2). It is to be expected that the chief effect of this change is on the sites of overconcentration. Thus, overconcentration should be found

---

to combine import surplus and product, the latter being calculated at current prices.

in private rather than in public services during the mandatory period. This is part of the resource effect, to which we shall return later.

d. The second world war years differ from the rest of the period in almost all respects. During the war, and because of it, Palestine had a surplus on current balance of payments, and so, presumably, did the Jewish sector, which became a considerable net exporter of services in the process. The 1940–45 data of Table 5.1 include in services all transactions with the Allied forces in the country, and therefore greatly overestimate the (negative) share of services in the import surplus. The British Army purchased large quantities of goods, and the construction and public works branch also supplied some of the military export. At the same time, the Jewish sector provided the army with much civilian manpower, as well as with electricity and water, trade, catering and medical services, etc. [2]

These wartime changes must have had two opposing effects on the volume of services: the conversion of the import surplus to an export surplus must by itself lead to a steep contraction in the service branches; while the fact that the Jewish sector became a net exporter of services operates in the opposite direction. The expected effect on the internal composition of services is for general government (which includes the War Department's civilian employees) and various personal services to expand.

Actual changes in the volume and composition of services are as expected, at least in direction: there is more overconcentration during the mandatory than during the State period, and in the first part of the latter than in the second part. Moreover, we find no general government overconcentration during the mandatory period; the private services—commerce and personal services—had greater weight, although even at this time there was overconcentration in 'other public services.' During the second world war we do in fact find both contraction in the total volume of services (compared with adjacent periods) and expansion in general government and some personal services. [3]

[2] For details see Jewish Agency, "The Occupational Structure of Jewish Earners," *Alon Statisti,* I (1946), pp. 16–52, *passim.* In 1945, there were 2,000 Jewish clerks, watchmen, and camp guards employed by the Army. Similarly, a considerable number of doctors and other professional persons joined the Services. For wartime changes in the balance of payments see R.R. Nathan, O. Gass, and D. Creamer, *Palestine: Problem and Promise,* Washington, 1946, p. 329.

[3] See Table 4.6 for 1943. In 1945 peacetime activity was resumed, although the Jewish sector was still a considerable exporter of services (Table 5.1 for 1946).

The volume of international trade

Importing and exporting usually require more inputs of trade, transportation and other business services than does dealing in local goods. During the State period the volume of foreign trade was not abnormal (compared with other countries), but in the 1930's it was considerable for the Jewish sector, and this may explain some of the sector's overconcentration in commerce at the time. In 1936 foreign trade came to 41 per cent [4] of national income, compared with 45 per cent of GNP in the Netherlands, 37 per cent in Norway, 33 per cent in Ireland, 32 per cent in Belgium, and lower rates in larger or less developed countries. When countries are ranked by level of development and population, it is found that the Israel figure is comparable to the five countries at the highest income level with the smallest population.[5] In 1954, the corresponding figure for Israel was 25 per cent, and in 1959 it was 22 per cent. [6]

Relations with the Arab sector

In Chapter 1 it was pointed out that during the mandatory period the Jewish sector was isolated from the Arab sector to an extent that justified its separate treatment as an economic entity, whose relations with the Arab sector (and the government sector—see Section 2 below) are part of foreign trade. Systematic data in money terms on these trade relations are found only in Gaathon, [7] for the single year 1936. According to this source, intersectoral trade was 15 per cent of the Jewish sector's total foreign trade,[8] and here also the Jewish sector had a current account deficit. Purchases from the Arab sector consisted mainly of agricultural produce, organic fertilizers, building materials, land,

---

[4] Calculated from the data underlying Table 5.1 as ½ (imports+exports) as per cent of national income.

[5] It has been found that the ratio foreign trade/GNP is higher in small than in large countries, and in developed than in less developed ones. See S. Kuznets, "Economic Growth of Small Nations," in *Economic Consequences of the Size of Nations* (ed. E.A.G. Robinson), London, 1960, pp. 14–32, and M. Michaely, *Foreign Trade and Capital Import in Israel*, Am Oved, 1963 (Hebrew), pp. 89 ff., Table 41.

[6] M. Michaely, *op. cit.*

[7] L. Gruenbaum (Gaathon), *National Income and Outlay in Palestine 1936*, Jerusalem, 1941, p. 19.

[8] About 15 per cent of imports, 18 per cent of exports, and 11 per cent of the import surplus.

dwelling services, and the services of Arab labour, especially in agriculture and in Haifa Port. The principal Jewish sales to the Arab sector were manufactures and electricity, and a small volume (LP 25,000) of professional—mostly medical—services. The value of goods includes a considerable input of trade services, apparently supplied mostly by the Jewish sector. Other sources confirm that the Arab sector made extensive use of the relatively advanced commercial facilities of the Jewish sector, for both intersectoral trade and imports. The Jewish sector was also active in the Middle East transit trade through Palestine. [9]

In general, intersectoral trade enabled the Jewish sector to reduce the employment share of agriculture, port services and construction, and to increase the employment shares of industry, commerce, and medical and other professional services.

Part of the overconcentration in trade and 'other public services' in the mandatory period can therefore be ascribed to the export of these services to the Arab sector. The Jewish sector was able to carry out this export because of the higher level of development and the occupational structure of its population, which gave it a comparative advantage in the supply of commercial and professional services. Intersectoral relations were artificially restricted by the hostility between the sectors, and by the Zionist ideology which tried to induce a 'normal' structure in the Jewish sector. If relations between the two sectors had been normal, and if simple criteria of economic profitability had been applied, there is no doubt that there would have been much more intersectoral trade.

During the second world war intersectoral trade was swallowed up by the much greater volume of similar (on the export side) trade with the armed forces stationed in Palestine.

2. GOVERNMENT SERVICES AND RESOURCES DURING THE MANDATE

The role of government

The structure and principles of the mandatory authorities' institutions had a marked effect on the share of public services in the Jewish sector. The Mandatary had a narrow conception of the functions of central

---

[9] Jewish Agency, *Statistical Handbook of Jewish Palestine, 1947*, Jerusalem, pp. 236 and 238–39. According to official data, transit trade accounted for 5 to 10 per cent of Palestine exports, and for a much smaller percentage of imports, before the second world war.

government, and failed to exploit available means of mobilizing resources.

The Jewish sector's institutions had a broad conception of the role of
government, which could not be fully realized owing to institutional and
resource limitations.

The principal 'sufferers' in this situation were the general government
services, and they were much less comprehensive than since the establishment of the State. Health and education services were less affected,
since ways were found to provide a fairly extensive supply despite the
fact that the central government allocated them only a small part of its
budget.

The evaluation of the economic and fiscal approach of the government, as reflected in its budgets, has been the subject of widespread
controversy in the economic and political literature. Nevertheless, it
is accepted that the practical results of this approach are to be seen in
the government's relatively small and narrowly applied contribution to
the country's economic development. This is not the place to discuss
whether the policy was intentionally designed to retard the development
of the country or of the Jewish sector, or whether it resulted from a
narrow definition of the role of government, and a cautious and con-
servative fiscal outlook—at that period, common to the mandatory and
the United Kingdom governments. [10] However that may be, the mandatory government was content to supply those services that had been
the traditional province of government for some decades past: internal
and external law and order, road-building and some elementary transportation and communication services, with only very limited provision of welfare and economic services. Moreover, this activity took
place within the rigid bounds of a balanced budget (or even a budget
surplus). It was only during the second world war that the government
extended its operations to price control and the supply of food and
other essential commodities.

Total government revenue from internal sources came to about 13
per cent of the national income in 1936/37; [11] external revenues were
very small, and in peacetime did not add more than 1 percentage point
to this amount. In all, the government employed about 2 per cent of
the labour force to provide its services (see Table 4.5). In peacetime,

---

[10] The different points of view are summarized in N. Halevi and R. Klinov-
Malul, *Development of the Israel Economy* (forthcoming), Chapter 2; the
principal bibliographical references will also be found there.

[11] Nathan, Gass, and Creamer, *op. cit.*, p. 342.

TABLE 5.3   *The Jewish Sector's Share in Central Government:
1931 and 1936*

		Total Palestine	Jewish Sector	Jewish sector as per cent of total Palestine
		Absolute numbers		
1.	Population in thousands			
	a. 1931	1,033	175	17
	b. 1936	1,389	404	29
2.	National income, 1936 (LP millions)	34.8	19.0	55
3.	Government activities, 1936 (LP millions)			
	a. Revenue	5.65	3.96	70
	b. Expenditure [a]	7.2	2.8	39
	c. Income originating [b]	3.7	0.9	24
4.	Government employment, 1931			
	a. In thousands	5.3	0.95	18
	b. As per cent of employed persons	1.9	1.7	**

[a] Expenditures on current and capital account (including depreciation). Includes government enterprises such as PTT and railways.
[b] Covers the same items as expenditure. The figure for Jewish sector is compensation of Jewish employees.
SOURCE: Population—Jewish Agency, *Statistical Handbook of Jewish Palestine 1947*, pp. 46–47.
National income—A.L. Gaathon, in *Encyclopaedia Hebraica*, Vol. VI, pp. 729–30.
Government activities—L. Gruenbaum (Gaathon), *National Income . . .*, *op. cit.*, pp. 90–91.
Government employment—from the sources of Table 4.5.

60 per cent of government expenditures went to defence and administration; about 25 per cent to public works (roads and railways); about 10 per cent to health and education; and about 7 per cent to various economic services. During the war the share of social and economic services was reduced even further. [12]

Table 5.3 illustrates the system of economic relations between the Jewish sector and the mandatory government in the 1930's. Several interesting features emerge from the table.

The Jewish sector received a greater share of government services than warranted by its contribution of labour (compare lines 6 and 7 with

[12] *Ibid.*

line 5). In foreign trade terminology it can be said that the Jewish sector was a net importer of government services. Additional data show that this import consisted mainly of postal and railway services. There seems to have been no net import of administrative services, and there was certainly none of economic and social services. [13] In general government also there was some substitution of skilled and unskilled labour between the Jewish and Arab sectors.

The Jewish sector paid (by purchases and by taxation) a disproportionately large amount for government services: 70 per cent (according to Gaathon's 1936 figures) and 55 per cent (according to data for 1944/45)—or much more than the 39 per cent of services it received. In foreign trade terminology, the government received in 1936 unilateral transfers of about LP 1.2 million from the Jewish sector (see Table 5.3).

During the second world war, more Jews were employed by government; however, if the relations with the armed forces are not taken into account, the peacetime picture is not substantially changed. [14]

The limited supply of government services was not enough for the Jewish community. The national aims of the community and its leaders' concept of the role of government dictated the creation of an autonomous governing machinery; this was designed to extend centralized activity to the fields of economic development and social services, as well as to organize the Jewish community into a political framework capable of achieving its political aims. The complete system of national and public institutions thus set up had its own peculiar character and also controlled some local authorities. These institutions—some of them established before the first world war—were the Jewish Agency, "a government co-existing with the mandatory government," which carried out almost all the functions of official government (it had foreign, political, and statistical departments, and of course departments dealing with immigration, the economy, resource mobilization and social services); the Jewish National Fund and the Foundation Fund whose main business was the acquisition of land and agricultural settlement; the Va'ad Leumi which acted as a sort of central municipal authority for the Jewish community, being a combination of departments for home affairs,

[13] L. Gruenbaum (Gaathon), *National Income* . . . ., *op. cit.*, pp. 90–91.

[14] For information on 1944/45 see Jewish Agency, *Statistical Handbook of Jewish Palestine 1947*, p. 392.

In this year the government received a relatively large sum in foreign aid. If these receipts are excluded, the Jewish share in government revenue is 6.5 per cent.

health, education, welfare, etc.; health organizations, of which the most important were Hadassah and the Histadrut Sick Fund; institutions for welfare and higher education; and local government institutions and various other trade and political associations.

The development of this institutional system is the principal factor behind the expansion of Jewish employment in general government from the early 1930's: at the beginning of the period, the branch accounted for about 1 per cent of employed persons (including Jews other than police employed by central government); at the termination of the Mandate the figure was about 4 per cent. [15] The growth of national quasi-governmental institutions gave general government continuity over the change of regime; the whole period thus gives the impression of normal growth—it is as though the country's government had passed though the same ideological evolution as did those in many other countries in the first half of the 20th century.

The resources at the disposal of the Jewish public sector [16]

In the mandatory period, more than at any other time, the scope and character of the Jewish public sector's activities was determined by the resources at its disposal. There is no doubt that resources constituted the effective restraint on the sector's activities, a much tighter restraint than normal conditions would have permitted. This is particularly striking when contrasted with the better-than-normal conditions of the public sector since the establishment of the State (see pp. 57–59). There were several reasons for the situation.

The Jewish sector paid 12 to 15 per cent of its national income to the central government: two thirds of the amount in the form of taxes, and the rest in direct payment for services. As seen, payments exceeded the value of services received by the sector.

The Jewish institutions had only limited powers of taxation (local government institutions and even the Va'ad Leumi were able to levy some property taxes), and for their other resources depended on voluntary contributions.

Only a small part of the country's capital imports accrued to the

---

[15] Table 4.9. See also Jewish Agency, "The Occupational Structure . . .," op. cit., p. 41.

[16] The data used in this section derive from Nathan, Gass, and Creamer, op. cit., Chapter 21, and from the chapters on government finance and the Jewish governing, educational, and health institutions in Jewish Agency, Statistical Handbook of Jewish Palestine 1947.

Jewish public sector; the bulk of the capital was brought by or transferred to private persons (Table 5.2). The Jewish sector, moreover, was not in a position to obtain international credit on a large scale.

Nevertheless, the Jewish institutions together succeeded in raising more than half as much as the central government, an amount far exceeding the sums spent by the central government on the supply of services to the Jewish sector. From 1920 to 1945 the central government raised about LP 100 million; in the same period, the Jewish sector contributed about LP 40 million to various national and public institutions, and about another LP 20 million to the Va'ad Leumi and Jewish local authorities (and the Jewish share in mixed local authorities). These amounts do not include the sums raised and spent by the Histadrut Sick Fund (about 15 per cent of public sector revenue in 1945). If these are also taken into account, we arrive at a figure of about LP 80 million, compared with the LP 100 million of the central government. About 85 per cent of the national institutions' revenues consisted of foreign grants, and the rest came from various (also mainly voluntary) sources. About 50 per cent of Va'ad Leumi and local government expenditures were financed by taxation, and a further 15 per cent by the direct sale of services. The Sick Fund's health services were financed by members' premiums, and some of the education services by direct sale. Only 4 per cent of the sector's total revenues were central government grants.

In 1945, the Jewish public sector had about LP 10.5 million at its disposal—about 13 per cent of the Jewish sector's national income in that year. If private expenditures on education and the expenditures of the Sick Fund are included, the figures are LP 13.5 million and 17 per cent, respectively. The supply of central government services to the Jewish sector adds another 7 to 8 per cent of national income. Altogether, the revenue of the Jewish public sector and its share of central government services come to less than half (as a proportion of national income) of the rate in the period of the State.

Most of the data cited here, in particular for national income, are for the end of the second world war and the last years of the mandate. This period saw a peak in the resources available to the Jewish sector during the mandate (both absolutely and relatively). In the 1930's resources were much more limited, as were the activities of the national and public institutions.

3. THE OCCUPATIONAL STRUCTURE OF IMMIGRATION

Over the entire period, about 70 per cent of the increase in Jewish population and labour force was due to immigration. The question arises of how the former occupational structure of immigrants affected the occupational and industrial structure of the country's labour force.

There is on the face of it no reason to suppose that the occupational structure which resulted from a random combination of Jewish minorities from all over the world should bear any resemblance to that required for the creation of a viable Jewish economy in Palestine. The word 'required' is used to indicate primarily a demand structure which must—unlike in the Diaspora—be supplied by the Jewish economy itself with the help of normal exchange relations with surrounding economies. It is possible to speak of a random combination because almost all immigration after 1939, and much of it even earlier, was unselective; complete communities (or their survivors) entered the country; they came for reasons connected with their countries of origin rather than because of any guidance (and certainly not vocational guidance) from Palestine. The pre-1939 immigration will be discussed later. Nevertheless, it is clear that even two quite different occupational structures must have a wide area in common; in order to pass from one to the other, only some of the immigrants need change their occupation.

We have so far assumed that the previous occupational structure has no effect on the new one, an assumption which is not valid *a priori*. In the short run, the actual occupational structure may depart from what is normal or desirable if special supply conditions arise in certain occupations. Shortages or oversupply of some occupations, which might not arise within the economy, might exist among the immigrants. Any oversupply is likely to persist longer in an occupation requiring long and specific training, and where experience counts. The greater the importance of any of these factors, the less inclined will people be to change their occupation; this is both for economic reasons—the high alternative cost of changing occupation, and the fact that new training and experience are not required in the old one—and for reasons of taste, habit, and security. The more difficult the conditions of economic integration in the country are (in any branch) the higher the alternative costs will be.

All this means that immigrants are prepared to work in their old occupation at a relatively low remuneration. A different situation is likely to arise when the development of an economic activity is held back because the supply of appropriately qualified manpower is inelastic —even though otherwise conditions in the country are favourable. If persons with the necessary qualifications immigrate, they are able to expand such branches without any loss of income.

The occupational structure of Israel's labour force is the result of a process of mutual adaptation: the immigrants adapt themselves to following their trade under new conditions and to the demand for it; and the consumer demand of both immigrants and the established population becomes adapted to the supply of services made possible by the occupational structure of immigration. The community and State institutions take account of both factors: on the one hand, they are interested in ensuring a 'healthy' economic structure, and in supplying an adequate volume of services (such as health and education); on the other hand, they are interested in the successful absorption of immigrants. These aims sometimes conflict.

The most striking feature of this process of adaptation is the marked change in the occupational structure of immigrants immediately after their arrival in the country. This has been discussed, for the mandatory period, by D. Horowitz, [17] while R. Bachi and others have treated the mandatory period and the mass immigration of 1948–52 together. From the 1954 Labour Force Survey it appears that in 1954 between 40 and 55 per cent of veteran employed persons and 50 to 70 per cent of new immigrants declared that they changed their occupation after immigrating. [18] The structure actually found in Palestine or Israel could have been achieved with less occupational mobility.

Before 1939, there were also some attempts to adapt immigrants' occupations to the country's requirements before they arrived. This is clear from the high proportion of agricultural workers among the pre-1939 immigrants,[19] which in no way reflected the occupational

---

[17] D. Horowitz, *The Economy of Palestine and its Development,* (revised edition), 1948, pp. 154–57.

[18] R. Bachi as quoted in A. Hovne, *The Labor Force in Israel,* FP, 1961, p. 45, Table 18, and in M. Sicron, *Immigration to Israel: 1948–1953,* FP and CBS Special Series No. 60, 1957, p. 119.

'Veterans' immigrated before, and 'new immigrants' after, the establishment of the State.

[19] Persons who declared that their occupation abroad was agriculture (in per cent of earners immigrating in the given period): 1919–23, 30 per cent; 1924–31, 20.6 per cent; 1932–38, 11.6 per cent; compare this with about 5 per cent after 1938. See M. Sicron, *op. cit.,* Statistical Supplement, p. 17, Table A26.

structure of Jews in the Diaspora, but resulted from deliberate pre-immigration training.

How far did the occupational structure of immigrants contribute to the country's services overconcentration at different times? Despite the evidence that many immigrants changed their occupation, there are signs that previous occupations played their part in the overconcentration in trade and the liberal professions.

Trade

Table 5.4 compares the proportion of merchants and other commerce workers among immigrant earners with the proportion of employed labour force in commerce (or whose occupation is 'trade'). Column (2) gives a crude measurement of the weight of the immigrant earners of

TABLE 5.4   *The Effect of Immigration on Employment in Commerce*

	Immigrants			Jewish employed persons		
Period	Immigrant earners		Year	Per cent in commerce	Per cent merchants[b]
	as per cent of all earners in the country[a]	per cent merchants[b]			
(1)	(2)	(3)	(4)	(5)	(6)
1919–23		6.9			
1924–31	56	9.2	1931	14.1	..
1932–38[e]	32[d]	15.8	1936	15.7	..
			1939	14.6	..
1939–45	10	19.4	1943	12.2	..
			1945	14.7	..
1946–47	3	1.8	1948	13.3	8.6
1948–55[e]	22	16.0	1955	14.0	11.7
1955–61	12	7.0	1961	12.3	8.9

[a] Immigrants arriving during the period, and earners in the country at the end of the period.
[b] In the occupational (as distinct from the industrial) classification.
[e] Most of those coming in this period had arrived by 1936.
[d] The figure appears to be understated.
[e] From 1.IX.48.
SOURCE: Immigrants—1955–61, CBS, *SAI 1963,* No. 14, p. 116, Table 9 (Migration). Other years, M. Sicron, *op. cit.* Statistical Supplement, Tables A26, A90 and A91.
        Employed persons—Table 4.6, and for occupation, CBS, *Registration of Population (8.XI.1948)* Part B, Special Series No. 53, p. 42, Table 23 and *SAI 1963,* No. 14, p. 510, Table 16 (Labour Force).

a given period in the end-of-period labour force. In interpreting the data it should be remembered that not all persons employed in commerce are 'merchants,' although most persons whose occupation is 'trade' are in fact employed in this branch. There is fair agreement between column (3) on the one hand, and columns (5) and (6) on the other, at least as regards the direction of the changes. The proportion of traders rose in the 1932–38 immigration, and at the same time the employment share of commerce rose from 1931 to 1936, despite the already high 1931 level. The wartime immigration apparently had a weaker effect [this is also seen in column (2)]. [20] The two series also agree for the later years. The high proportion of immigrant earners whose occupation was trade (mainly in the period of mass immigration) led to a higher proportion of 'merchants and salesmen,' and a moderate rise in the employment share of commerce. The subsequent decline in the labour force rates was accompanied by a similar decline among immigrants. Immigration can explain about half of the change in the employment share of commerce in 1932–38 and in 1948–55; for 1948–54, Bachi finds that trade is the principal occupation given up by immigrants after arriving in the country,[21] and this emphasizes the incompleteness of the explanation. Immigration explains only a very small part of the decline which took place in the employment share of commerce from 1955 to 1961. [22]

The liberal professions and public services

There was a high proportion of professional and technical persons among immigrants in all periods (Tables 5.5 and 5.6), especially in 1932–45 and 1955–61.

Immigration was the principal and almost the only source of professional manpower for the Jewish sector of Palestine. During the mandatory period several institutions of higher learning already existed; the most important were the Hebrew University which granted its first humanities degrees in 1932, and natural sciences degrees in 1935, and the Institute of Technology in Haifa (founded in 1925); there were also several teachers' training colleges. In 1945 there were about 2,000 students at all these institutions, [23] and they supplied only a few of the

---

[20] See also pp. 136–37 below.

[21] M. Sicron, *op. cit.*, p. 9 (Introduction by R. Bachi), and p. 119.

[22] The calculations are very crude and are not brought here. In principle they consist of computing what the employment share of commerce would be if the entire change in share were due to immigration.

[23] Jewish Agency, *Statistical Handbook of Jewish Palestine 1947*, pp. 336, 341.

TABLE 5.5   *Professional Immigrants by Period of Immigration*

(per cent of all immigrant earners)

	1919–47	1932–45	1950–61	1950–55
Total	11.5	14.2	11.7	8.4
Medicine	3.4	4.3	3.6	2.3
Engineering	1.4	2.1	2.4	1.5
Education	2.7	2.6	2.3	2.1
Religion	1.6	2.3	0.7	0.8
Law	.. [a]	.. [a]	0.7	0.7
Other	2.4	2.9	2.0	1.0

[a] Included in 'other'.
SOURCE: M. Sicron, *Immigration to Israel, 1948–1953*, FP and CBS Special Series No. 60, Statistical Supplement, 1957, Tables A26, and A91. For column (3), CBS, *SAI 1963*, No. 14, pp. 114–15, Table 8.

country's professionals. For several professions, the most important of which was medicine, there was no possibility of training in the country before the end of the Mandate. Immigration thus also provides the explanation for overconcentration in such jobs. Overconcentration was at its most serious at the end of the 1930's, but was still a problem after

TABLE 5.6   *The Effect of Immigration on Employment in Liberal Professions*

Immigrants		Jewish Employed Persons		
Period	Per cent in liberal professions [a]	Year	Per cent in 'other public services'	Per cent 'technical and professional workers' [a]
(1)	(2)	(3)	(4)	(5)
1919–1923	10.6			
1924–1931	7.1	1931	13.1	..
1932–1938	14.2	1936	11.4	..
		1939	13.8	..
1939–1945	14.3	1945	13.2	..
1946–1947	8.8	1948	11.2	10.0
1948–1955	8.6	1955	13.2 [b]	10.9
1955–1961	15.4	1961	15.6	12.2

[a] In the occupational (as distinct from the industrial) classification.
[b] 1954.
SOURCE: See Table 5.4.

the war. The liberal professions require the longest training of all occupations, and in some cases the training is highly specialized, and it is difficult to find a suitable alternative use.

Clearly, the system of health, education, legal, engineering, and architectural services established in the country is unimaginable without the professional immigrants. This statement can be rephrased, as regards at least some of the professions: the will and the necessity to absorb as many as possible of the professionals in their own occupations spurred the community's institutions to set up these systems. Nevertheless the extensive health services, already established before the war, could not absorb all the doctors and other medical workers who immigrated. According to estimates made at the time, there were more than 3.5 doctors per 1,000 inhabitants (or about 280 persons per doctor—see Table 5.8). In addition there was one dentist for every 700 inhabitants (in the US there were 2,000 persons per dentist in 1950). [24] It is not surprising that the government eventually suspended the issue to doctors of licences to practise.[25]

The problem of oversupply of professional manpower is described in the following terms by Hanoch: "The usual correlation between levels of education and income was also low in the pre-State Jewish community. Many of the immigrants had secondary or higher education, and the usual relative scarcity of people with such education, and the consequent premium placed on it, did not exist. Many of the educated immigrants abandoned their professions and took up manual labor. And since their previous training was not used, it received no monetary compensation." [26] During the mandatory period, too, the relative incomes of public services workers were low, as can be seen in Table 4.10. The low incomes, the exodus to other occupations (some women, indeed, leaving the labour force altogether), the failure to employ more doctors despite the extensive health system—all these are evidence that in many of the professions the community had passed saturation point.

It was only with the establishment of the State and mass immigration

[24] G.J. Stigler, *Trends in Employment in the Service Industries*, NBER, Princeton, 1956, p. 108, Table 39.

[25] The information in this paragraph is from Jewish Agency, "The Occupational Structure . . .," *op. cit.*, pp. 9, 38.

[26] Giora Hanoch, "Income Differentials in Israel," *Fifth Report 1959 and 1960*, FP, Jerusalem, 1961, p. 43.
See also Jewish Agency, "The Occupational Structure . . .," *op. cit.*, and L. Gruenbaum (Gaathon), *Outlines for a Development Plan for Palestine*, Jewish Agency, 1946, p. 85.

that the already high saturation level could be raised. [27] As demand rose, there was a sharp drop in the proportion of liberal professions among immigrant earners, at a time when the country's own supply of professionals (other than teachers) was still small. It is probable that some of those who had left their professions during the mandatory period returned at this time, but there was almost no increase in the employment share of 'other public services' from 1945 to 1955 (Table 5.6). Hanoch writes about the radical change in the situation: "from a relative abundance of persons with secondary and higher education, and of experts, there developed a quite serious shortage, and the necessity of encouraging a large number of persons to enter the professions served as an impetus for increasing the wages received by those with education and skills." [28] This shift is also reflected in our data by the rise in the product-worker ratio (see Table 4.10). A marked expansion in other public services began in 1955 and has continued until 1961—once more accompanied by an increase in the proportion of professional immigrants.

The fact that 'other public services' began to grow only in the second half of the State period is susceptible of several explanations; it is, however, difficult to avoid the impression that the coincidence of timing in the movement of the two series shows a causal relationship. As we have seen (p. 68), the economy has become less dependent, at least at the margin, on foreign-trained professionals—other than doctors. Nevertheless they are still an important element of professional manpower, and this is to-day still likely to affect the level of the country's public services.

The proportion of professional immigrants was important in determining the volume of public services in the Jewish sector of Palestine and in Israel throughout the period. In the mandatory period (and in medical services in other periods also) there was a surplus of manpower after extensive services had been set up. In the following section we shall briefly survey some other aspects of the volume of 'other public services.'

---

[27] See the discussion in Section 4 of this chapter.

[28] Giora Hanoch, *op. cit.*, p. 44. On the shortage of professional manpower in the early years of the State see also M. Sicron, *op. cit.*, p. 119.

4. EDUCATION AND HEALTH

Our discussion so far has been in terms of manpower supply and resources available to the Jewish sector. In order to round off the picture,
we shall examine several features of the development of the educational
and health services (see also of Sections 3 and 4 in Chapter 3).

Education

About 6 per cent of employed persons worked in education in 1931,
about 4.5 per cent in 1945, and over 7 per cent in 1961. If *yeshivot*
are excluded, the figures are, respectively, 4.3 per cent, 3.7 per cent, and
6.7 per cent. (Table 4.9). During the mandatory period, and *a fortiori*
since the establishment of the State, these figures are higher than those
found in other countries.

Table 5.7 describes the Jewish educational system in the country
throughout the period. [29] There was some decline in the percentage of
population in the 15–19 age-group [30] (the candidates for education) in
the early 1930's, and the figure was around 25 per cent until mass
immigration. Only in recent years did the population become younger
than usual in the more developed countries. In the first part of our
period the proportion of school-age population was not high, and may
even have been lower than in countries at the same level of development.

The proportion of the age-group attending school rose from slightly
under three quarters in the 1930's to slightly over three quarters after
the second world war. There was a marked decline in the attendance
rate at the time of mass immigration, but since 1952 there has been a
continuous increase, until in 1961 more than 85 per cent of the age-
group attended school. The high attendance rate during the mandatory
period is notable because it was achieved in the absence of a compulsory
education law, and because parents were required to defray directly
a large part of the cost of primary education—let alone secondary,
which parents must still pay for, wholly or in part. The rate is undoubtedly higher than that found in other countries at the same level
of development, and is explained by the high proportion of Europeans
among immigrants and in the population, by their high educational

---

[29] The data of this table differ from those of Table 3.6. See the notes to the
table.

[30] The educational system in this country does not include 19-year olds. This
grouping is dictated by the available statistics.

TABLE 5.7   *The Jewish Educational System: Selected Years*[a]

	1931	1939	1945	1951	1957	1961
A. *Absolute figures*						
1. Population aged 5–19 (thousands)	47.3	110.1	135.3	353.9	513.9	607.9
2. Pupils[b] (thousands)	34.2	79.2	105.7	231.2	414.4	522.0
3. Teachers[b]	1,669	3,602	5,388	10,880	15,627	21,862
B. *Per cent*						
4. 5–19 age group/population	27.9	24.7	24.6	25.7	29.2	31.5
5. Pupils/5–19 age group (2÷1.)	72.3	72.0	78.0	65.3	80.6	85.9
6. Pupils/population (4.×5.)	20.2	17.8	19.2	16.8	23.5	27.1
C. *Ratios*						
7. Pupils per teacher (2÷3)	20.1	22.0	19.6	21.2	26.5	24.0
8. Per cent of teachers in population (6÷7)	1.00	0.81	0.98	0.79	0.89	1.13

[a] Calendar years for population data and school-years (September–June) for education data.
[b] Kindergartens and all schools (i.e. excluding 'higher education'). For the state period 'other institutions' are also excluded.
SOURCE: 1931, 1939 and 1945—Population data: CBS, *Jewish Population (1931–1954)*, Special Series No. 37, Tables 3 and 4.
    Education data—Jewish Agency, *Statistical Handbook of Jewish Palestine 1947*, pp. 334–37.
    1951, 1957 and 1961—Chapters on Population and Education of various issues of *SAI*.

standards, and by the strong demand for educational services resulting from these qualities. [31] The decline in attendance which occurred in the early years of the State was due to the change in the demographic structure and to the organizational difficulties of coping with the tremendous influx of school-age children. The enactment of the compulsory education law, the reorganization of the school system, and the increase

[31] Close to 90 per cent of immigrants from 1918 to 1948 came from Europe. (M. Sicron, *op. cit.*, p. 28). See N. Halevi and R. Klinov-Malul, *op. cit.*, on the high educational standards of the population and immigrants during the mandatory period.

in grants for various forms of secondary education made it possible to reach a very high attendance rate by the end of the 1950's.

These two factors taken together show that the proportion of the whole population attending school reached 27 per cent in recent years, although it had never exceeded 20 per cent during the mandatory period, and even dropped to 18 per cent in the early 1950's. This change entails not only an increased demand for educational services, but also reduces the proportion of population from which educational staff can be drawn.

The pupil-teacher ratio was fairly stable at a low level of around 20 pupils per teacher until after the period of mass immigration. By the end of the 1950's it had risen considerably, but in recent years it dropped despite the continuing rise in the proportion of school-children in the population. During the mandatory period the ratio was low because the population was scattered in small settlements, because of the 'balkanization' inherent in the political stream system,[32] and perhaps because of a desire to use the large supply of teachers to provide higher standards. The rise in the pupil-teacher ratio reflected the difficulties which arose from the enormous expansion of the school-system after 1951. The recent moderate decline in the ratio reflects the desire to intensify the educational services, once the initial difficulties had been overcome.

All these factors are reflected in line 8 of Table 5.7, which shows the education burden undertaken by the Jewish sector. The relatively heavy burden of the mandatory period was due mainly to the low pupil-teacher ratio; in recent years the burden has increased despite the decline in the pupil-teacher ratio, owing to the rise in the proportion of school-children.

Health

Over the period the employment share of health services rose moderately, from the 3 to 4 per cent of the mandatory period to about 4.5 per cent in 1961. We saw that in 1961 there was a relatively large number of doctors (per head of population), a small number of hospital beds, and a large number of doctors' visits. Table 5.8 shows that this was so throughout, although to a greater degree during the mandatory period than later: during the Mandate the number of inhabitants per doctor was lower, and there were more visits to and by doctors. The number of beds for mental patients was apparently lower, relatively, than

---

[32] Until 1951, schools were organized in three streams: labour, religious and general (i.e. unpolitical).

TABLE 5.8   *Medical Services: Selected Years*

	1930	1938	1945	1951	1957	1961
1. Persons per doctor	283	207 [a]	267	438	463 [b]	397
2. Doctors' visits per insured person [c]	11.3	9.5	9.4	8.0	8.6 [c]	9.3
3. Number of hospital beds per inhabitant [d]	..	(2–2.5) [e]	..	3.2	3.1	3.1
4. Visits per doctor (thousands, 1.×2.)	3.2	2.0	2.5	3.5	4.0	3.7

[a] 1936.
[b] 1956.
[c] In Histadrut Sick Fund.
[d] General hospitals.
[e] Calculated on the basis of Hadassah and Histadrut Sick Fund, whose 900 hospital beds are about 2 per thousands.

SOURCE: 1930, 1938, 1945—
        Number of doctors: Jewish Agency, "The Occupational Structure of Jewish Earners", *Alon Statisti*, Vol. I, 1–6, June 1946. pp. 146, 156 and 165.
        Other data: Jewish Agency, *Statistical Handbook of Jewish Palestine 1947*, pp. 346–50.
        1951, 1957, 1961—CBS, *SAI 1963*, No. 14, pp. 146, 156, 165 (Health).

since the establishment of the State. In the early period almost all public health services were financed by the Histadrut Sick Fund and Hadassah; since the establishment of the State, however, the central government has assumed part of the burden, and today is responsible for one third of health service expenditure. It is difficult to make an objective assessment of the health needs of the Jewish population in both periods. A very crude index of efficiency (line 4 of Table 5.8) shows that doctors were less efficient during the mandatory period than later. The rise in health services employment since the end of the Mandate stems from the increased volume of the general services supplied by the State: the decline in the employment *share* was accompanied by a rise in efficiency.

5. BULGING IN SERVICES

'Bulging' is the name we have given to an increase in an economy's volume of services which is due to obstacles which prevent the development of a normal branch structure. A description of the phenomenon and of its causes is to be found in, for example, the following passage:

"Thus, in underdeveloped countries, with limited opportunities for productive employment, the supply of labor for personal services, and for certain types of petty trade, transportation, communication, etc., is quite large. The share of the labor force engaged in these subdivisions of the S sector, often including government, would be larger than in the more developed countries." A normal structural development, therefore, is one where industrial expansion precedes expansion in services. Services can be said to grow normally only when their growth coincides with, or follows, industrialization. [33] That bulging occurs in service industries is explained by the ease with which new manpower can be absorbed, and which contrasts with the great difficulty met with in expanding the absorptive capacity of manufacturing, particularly in underdeveloped countries. Services which experience bulging are those which require little basic investment, little production and marketing organization, and little technical knowledge—all in comparison with the requirements of manufacturing; the market situation is eased for such services because there is neither the problem of exporting, nor the competition of imports. A sudden increase in manpower supply, beyond the country's normal rate of growth will thus at first lead to increased employment in services; capital, and organizational and technical knowledge required for industrial expansion and the absorption of new manpower will be found only somewhat later. The phenomenon is likely to be of relatively short duration if its principal cause is a sudden growth of labour force, assisted by a lack of flexible and rapid means of industrial expansion. But bulging can also persist as a stage of economic growth.

Many students of growth have described a situation of 'limited scope for productive employment' as an economic bottleneck which prevents undeveloped countries from entering a dynamic growth process accompanied by industrialization and the productivization of agriculture. Most investigators have found that eliminating the bottleneck requires drastic and exogenous action or events. Such an event, which, in the open trade conditions of earlier periods, could well have been a revolutionary technical invention, must in modern times apparently consist of large-scale and deliberate investment operations, protection against foreign competition, agrarian reform, and so forth. Before the appearance of such an exogenous event or planned action, or during a period when any action taken is inadequate, or before it has borne fruit, we are likely to find services employment expanding. This happens because the

[33] S. Kuznets, *Countries,* pp. 16 and 32.

product per worker in agriculture declines, and disguised unemployment appears in agriculture and spreads to the services; this disguised unemployment is in turn caused by soil exhaustion and population growth. Where this happens, there is frequently a rise in the rate of natural increase, owing to improved health services. This puts increasing pressure on employment and worsens the bulging. Such bottlenecks can of course persist for some time.

The above description of bulging suggests the theoretical conclusion that the product-worker ratio of affected service industries will be low. This in fact is usual, both in short-run bulging, and when the condition is more persistent. But it is not necessarily so; a situation in which the product-worker ratio of services is above the national average, at least for a short time, can easily be envisaged. It may be the result of a very low income level in agriculture, compared to which any other occupation will bring greater rewards; it can also occur when the principle of economic profitability dictates that the economy should begin by expanding services—such as transportation and trade—and exploit any opportunity there may be of exchanging agricultural produce for foreign manufactures. In this way a costly process of industrialization can be avoided, or at least postponed; the standard of living can rise faster than would be possible during attempts to industrialize; and the product-worker ratio in the expanding branches can be considerably above the national average. In such circumstances, services overconcentration consists only in a departure from the path of development found in most economies: that is, services expand before industrialization. [34]

The quotation at the beginning of this section (p. 131) listed the branches susceptible to bulging. Mention should also be made of bulging in government services: here the process is explained mainly by the readiness of governments to find an easy solution for unemployment, in particular of new, partly educated, classes.

What has so far been said enables us to list the following symptoms of bulging in services:

a. The high level of services employment found in undeveloped countries, preceded by a period of rapid population growth.

b. The rising employment-share of services in undeveloped and developing countries which precedes industrialization and is accompanied by a rapid population growth.

---

[34] This process can also be the first stage of bulging which will eventually lead to a decline in the product-worker ratio.

c. The decline in the employment share of services at the height of accelerated industrialization (the emergence from bulging, and the absorption of workers in productive branches).

d. The product-worker ratio can, as we have seen, be variously affected by bulging. [35] Nevertheless a relatively low product-worker ratio can certainly be a sign of bulging.

The empirical study of these phenomena as a rule requires a specific approach for each country, and it is difficult to find comprehensive statistical tests. We have made one test of a very general character, and despite its many limitations it does perhaps lead to a conclusion of some sort. We compiled a table (not presented here) of deviations from the regression line of the product-worker ratios of various countries, corresponding to the table of employment share deviations (Table 3.4). Comparison of the two tables shows whether or not there is any connexion between bulging and the product-worker ratio. The predicted connexion between the deviations of employment share and of product-worker ratio was found in 24 out of the 36 countries for which we had information. In other words, overconcentration of employment was connected with a low product-worker ratio, and conversely, absence of deviation in one indicator went with absence of deviation in the second. In 12 of the countries there was no such relationship. Of the 24 countries where the prediction was borne out, 13 combined overconcentration of employment with a low product-worker ratio. The reservations as regards the use of regression lines for product-worker ratio hold good also in the present instance. [36]

Let us trace developments in several countries in which various investigators have found bulging.

Kuznets mentions Cuba, Mexico, and India as exceptions in which the employment share of services rose before industrialization. [37] For Mexico, the explanation has been provided by another investigator, who evaluates the situation as one of bulging. Discussing the marked rise in the employment share of services from 1940 to 1955, A.G. Jaffe writes: "the increase in the so-called service and white-collar industries in

---

[35] For example, in some undeveloped countries where there is bulging in personal services, itinerant trading and the like, the relatively low incomes of the surplus population may be offset by the incomes of a small but wealthy 'merchant prince' class supplying similar services.

[36] In addition, some of the results may be spurious: for example, if the share of employment, but not of product, is overstated, the data could show both overconcentration of employment and a low product-worker ratio.

[37] S. Kuznets, *Countries*, p. 32.

Mexico and elsewhere simply reflects the fact that the population of working-force age has increased more rapidly than have the job opportunities in industries producing physical goods. This is implicit in the fact that so many of these services and white-collar industries pay lower than average wages." [38] Jaffe's data, and those of Kuznets, show that from 1900 to 1950 the employment share of services in Mexico rose by 16 percentage points to double the starting level. Most of the increase (11 percentage points) was concentrated in the period 1935–50, but the rise also continued subsequently. Over the period there was almost no change in the share of the M sector (industry and construction) which remained at a low level. In the second quarter of the century the growth of population became very rapid, doubling from 1930 to 1957. [39]

The situation in Cuba is similar. Here it is reflected in a considerable overconcentration of employment in services, judged by the income-level criterion. (See Table 3.4). From 1919 to 1943 the services employment share rose from 31 per cent to 44 per cent, while the share of the M sector dropped by 5 percentage points. Here also, population growth was accelerated, and the population grew by 2.7 per cent per annum from 1919 to 1931. [40]

Similar situations arising from the same causes are found by Jaffe in Puerto Rico, and by Brown in Japan. [41]

In several countries—Australia, New Zealand, and perhaps Finland and Norway—we find the services employment share rising during a lull in the industrialization process. Clark has this to say on Australia and New Zealand: ". . . after this, the industrial proportion fell slightly until the 1930's, the development of both countries in the period being predominantly agricultural. More recently, there has been a rapid but artificial development of industry." [42] During the transition period from the beginning of the 20th century to the 1930's the employment share of services rose steeply in both countries: from 40 per cent to 47 per cent in Australia, and from 37 per cent to 46 per cent in New Zealand. At the

---

[38] A.G. Jaffe, *People, Jobs, and Economic Development,* The Free Press of Glencoe, Illinois, 1959, pp. 264–65.

[39] *Ibid.* p. 147 and S. Kuznets, *Countries,* Appendix Table 3.

[40] S. Kuznets, *loc. cit.* The figures on population growth are from UN, *Demographic Yearbook 1962,* Table 7.

[41] A.G. Jaffe, *op. cit.,* p. 104, and E.H.P. Brown, *The Economics of Labor,* Yale University Press, New Haven, 1962, pp. 84–85.
Jaffe speaks of the close connexion in the very short run between population growth and employment in services.

[42] Colin Clark, *The Conditions of Economic Progress,* London, 1957, p. 502.

same time, the employment share of manufacturing declined in New Zealand and remained steady in Australia. In both countries the employment share of agriculture declined. The population grew rapidly at about 2 per cent annually. The deliberate policy of industrialization followed by both governments from the mid-1930's on undoubtedly arose from the pressure of agricultural depression and of population growth. Until the mid-thirties, such employment was found in services expansion. In both countries, the share of industry again rose and the rise of the services employment share was arrested from the mid-1930's until after the second world war. During the period of bulging, the product-worker ratio of services rose, but only just, beyond a ratio of 1.00. [43]

A similar situation, also discussed by Clark, [44] is found in Denmark in the period 1900–30, when the share of agriculture declined and industry stagnated, while the share of services rose from 30 per cent to 39 per cent. This rise was almost entirely arrested when industrialization was renewed in the period 1930–50. The picture in Norway is almost identical. Neither Denmark nor Norway show any sign of population pressure from natural increase, but in both cases there is migration from agriculture.

The expansion of services rather than industry in developing colonial societies is discussed by Epstein in an article on the economic development of a Far Eastern colonial society. Her description of trade and transportation suggests that the product-worker ratio of these branches is relatively high. [45]

Some of the conditions for bulging have existed in Israel within the period under review. The first, seen throughout, is an unparalleled growth of population and labour force. The annual rate of growth of

---

[43] *Ibid.* The data on Australia are from p. 510 and on New Zealand, from p. 517. See also S. Kuznets, *Countries,* Appendix Tables 2 to 6.

[44] Colin Clark, *op. cit.,* p. 503.

[45] Epstein arrives at the following generalization: "It appears to be a feature of small-scale colonial societies ... to invest in tertiary industries such as transport and retail services, rather than in manufacturing ventures. This can be easily explained by the smallness of the home market .... Tolai have too little know-how of world markets to try to produce manufactured articles for export. Thus investment in service industries, ..., which by their very nature are protected from external competition, provides the only economic outlet for their capital." ("European Contact and Tolai Economic Development: A Schema of Economic Growth," *Economic Development and Cultural Change,* Vol. XI, No. 3 Part I, April 1963, p. 304).

the Jewish population was 8.5 per cent between 1922 and 1948 and 7.6 per cent between 1948 and 1961;[46] there were, however, fluctuations reflecting the different waves of immigration. Growth was particularly rapid in the mid-1920's, in 1932–37 and in 1948–51; in each of these periods the Jewish population more than doubled.[47] The mandatory period and the period of the State each showed some of the other conditions necessary for bulging.

Throughout the period, the small Israel economy faced considerable difficulties owing to the shortage of capital, the lack of experience and technical knowledge, and the small size of the market. During the mandatory period these difficulties were enhanced by the restrictive economic policy of the mandatory government, which failed to give active assistance to development and provided only limited tariff protection against foreign competition. The Jewish institutions at that time had only limited resources at their disposal and this restricted their direct development activities (and prevented them from absorbing surplus immigrant labour on their staffs). The second world war had provided special conditions for expanding industrial employment, although it had at the same time seriously damaged the important citrus branch. In 1948, political sovereignty created the possibility of easing some of these difficulties. The government initiated a policy of extensive development, helped by the relatively plentiful resources at its disposal; stringent import controls were imposed, which made industrial and agricultural development easier; and the legal and institutional restrictions inherited from an unsympathetic regime were removed. Furthermore, the government's control of a larger share of the economy's resources, and its declared full employment policy encouraged work-seekers to turn to the government apparatus, and the government itself to use this apparatus to relieve the pressure of unemployment.

Nevertheless, the rapid population growth seems to have been the decisive element in the appearance of bulging in Israel until the mid-1950's. The other factors had less effect. This is confirmed by the high unemployment rates that prevailed from 1948 to 1954. It was only when immigration slackened that the government's absorption and development efforts and the country's rapid economic development succeeded in creating employment demand conditions favourable to a weakening of the bulging process. The ease with which the government was able to absorb workers after the establishment of the State in itself gave a

[46] UN, *Demographic Yearbook 1962,* Table 7.
[47] CBS, *SAI 1963,* No. 14, p. 18.

further impetus to bulging, and was liable to change its structure. The evidence of contemporary writers and of currently available data indicates that bulging occurred in trade and personal services up to the mid-1950's, and in general government during the first half of the State's existence.

The existence of bulging during the mandatory period is discussed by Gaathon. [48] In the development plan he stresses the need for placing the economy on a wider base of productive branches in order to absorb the excess services employment. He also expresses the hope that the decline in the volume of services during the second world war was due to a real extension of the economic foundations into other branches, as well as being inherent in the wartime situation.

In the State period, bulging and its symptoms were found mainly in the early years. A group of investigators at work in 1955 linked excess employment in services with the low labour force participation rate, and explained both in two ways, one of which was: "The Israel economy has not yet been able to provide productive work opportunities for a large part of its recent and rapid population increase ... ; to a degree, services, including government employment, play the role in Israel which is played by agriculture in most underdeveloped countries—that of the concealer of underemployment." [49] Similar statements can be found elsewhere. [50] It is difficult to ignore the unanimity of the authorities writing on the first half of the State period.

Trade

As stated, the employment share of trade exceeded the international norm throughout the period until the mid-1950's; there was then a steep decline, beginning at the latest in 1955, which ran counter to trends found in normal conditions in other countries. This is strong evidence

---

[48] L. Gruenbaum (Gaathon), *National Income and Outlay in Palestine 1936*, Jerusalem, 1941, p. 25, and *Outlines for a Development Plan for Palestine*, Jewish Agency, Jerusalem, 1946, pp. 85, 98, 101–102.

[49] Economic Advisory Staff, *The Israel Economy in 1954*, Jerusalem, July 1955, p. 57 (mimeograph).

[50] S. Riemer, "Wages in Israel," *Encyclopaedia Hebraica*, Vol. VI, pp. 804–805, D. Patinkin, *The Israel Economy: The First Decade*, FP, Jerusalem, 1960, p. 35, and Bank of Israel, *Annual Report 1955*.

It should be noted that the authors so far cited relied on the results of the first (1954) Labour Force Survey, which showed a much lower percentage of labour force employed in services (especially in trade) than did the estimates for the industrial distribution of earners of the preceding years.

that there had been bulging in trade. Further confirmation is found in the short-run changes: the employment share rose in the period 1931–36, a time of mass immigration; it declined slightly in the late 1930's; with the virtual cessation of immigration during the second world war it declined further; after the war, the share rose again under the pressure of demobilization and renewed immigration. After the establishment of the State, the income-level rose rapidly, while the employment share of trade remained fairly constant during 1948–1954/55, and this suggests some weakening in the bulging process at this time.[51]

A glance at the occupational structure of immigrants shows that when there was a high proportion of traders among immigrants there were also symptoms of bulging. This complementarity is clear: absorption difficulties encourage the new immigrant to stay in his old occupation. The combination of immigrants' occupational structure with absorption difficulties in the productive branches during the mandatory period, is described as follows: "In this branch [trade] we have reached a saturation point, and from now on [development] depends largely on the composition of immigration, and on the efforts of the economic leadership of the Jewish community to direct the manpower arriving in the country . . . to primary and secondary occupations." [52]

The information available on product-worker ratio in trade shows a high ratio in 1936, and a lower figure in 1945 and until the middle 1950's. In 1955 the ratio begins to rise, though without reaching its 1936 level (see Table 4.10). The figures (except for the 1936 ratio) are consistent with incipient bulging. The high ratio for 1936 may be explained by analogy with the examples discussed earlier of bulging associated with a high product-worker ratio. Free international trading in goods may have created temporary conditions of greater profitability for investment in trade. The high product-worker ratio was also a reflection of the low incomes in other branches—especially agriculture— at the time. Gaathon explains this in terms of "a large number of shops with a small turnover, and a high mark-up" [53]—an explanation founded

---

51 This conclusion cannot of course be upheld if the Nizan estimates are accepted. In this case it must be said that bulging was in full swing in commerce during the period, but disappeared as soon as the stream of mass immigration dried up, so that by 1954 there were almost no signs of bulging left. See note 19 on p. 86.

52 Jewish Agency, "The Occupational Structure of Jewish Earners," *Alon Statisti,* Vol. I, 1–6, June 1946, p. 34.

53 L. Gruenbaum (Gaathon), *National Income and Outlay in Palestine 1936,* Jerusalem, 1941, p. 16.

on the existence of market imperfections. Other factors, already mentioned, were the import surplus effect, the transit trade, the fact that at the time most of those engaged in trade brought some capital to the country with them; all these can explain a temporary overconcentration in the branch, not accompanied by a decline in the product-worker ratio.

Personal services

Bulging apparently also occurred in some personal services, such as restaurants and cafes and domestic services. There are data which show that the employment share of catering was lower after the establishment of the State than in the mandatory period. The decline in the share of domestic services is often associated with economic development, and it is therefore difficult to decide whether the initial level was too high. However, the 10 to 11 per cent employment share in personal services until 1954 (including kibbutzim—without the kibbutzim, the figure is about 8 per cent, from the late 1930's) suggest that there was some bulging. The employment share of personal services declined steeply after 1954, and the product-worker ratio was higher after than before the State was established; these facts support the conclusion. [54]

General government

There is no evidence of bulging in general government during the mandatory period, and the conditions for it were in fact lacking. On the other hand, general government was the principal point of overconcentration in the early years of the State. The data used in Chapter 4 do not tell us much about the development of the employment share during the State period. Presumably, some increase took place in 1948 with the transfer of authority, before the Registration of Population carried out at the end of the year. There was a further increase from 1948 to 1954 (from about 7.7 per cent to 8.6 per cent). Most of the rise took place in central government, the share of local government remaining almost the same, and the share of national institutions etc. perhaps even declining slightly. On the face of it, bulging must therefore be sought in central government.

Table 5.9 shows the development of the civil service during the period of the State. The data cover employees who would come under

[54] The rise in the number of domestic servants during the mandatory period is discussed in L. Gruenbaum (Gaathon), *Outlines for a Development Plan for Palestine*, Jewish Agency, Jerusalem, 1946, p. 98.

TABLE 5.9   *The Civil Service: Selected Years*

	31.3.49	31.3.52	31.3.55	31.3.61[a]
A. All central government employees	12,683	33,334	38,310	47,403
B. Per 1,000 inhabitants				
Total	12.1	20.8	21.9	21.7
Ports, railways and PTT	3.2	5.3	5.0	5.0
Total (excluding enterprises)	8.9	15.5	16.9	16.7
Police	3.4	4.0	4.3	3.5
Administration	2.9	4.9	5.7	5.6
Economic services	1.6	3.8	3.4	3.4
Social services	1.0	2.8	3.5	4.2

[a] Not the same breakdown as in Table 3.10 where some employees were excluded for the comparison with Great Britain.

SOURCE: Civil Service Commission, *Second, Seventh,* and *Eleventh Reports,* and *State Budgets* (for some of the police data).

other branches in our classification, and thus differ from those of Chapter 4. The principal expansion (absolutely, and in relation to population) took place in the period 1949–52; this was followed by a further small rise from 1952 to 1955, when the highest level in terms of per cent of population was reached. Between 1949 and 1955, the ratio of government employees to population almost doubled. This may be interpreted in two ways: first, the new government naturally consolidated its apparatus within a few years, in accordance with its social and economic outlook; a period of four years seems very plausible for this purpose. The second interpretation is that there was bulging, and this is also supported by many of the features of the time—mass immigration, high unemployment, and the readiness of the government to resort to deficit financing. The table shows that there were indications of bulging in two areas of government activity. The first is police, whose employment share rose until 1955, but later declined to its initial 1948 level. In fact, the police reached their highest absolute number in 1955. In recent years we have heard much of a shortage of policemen and recruitment difficulties. Clearly, there were no such difficulties in the earlier period. The second fact which suggests bulging is the high employment share of general administration. This accounts for one half of government employment (other than police and enterprises); the comparable figure for Great Britain is one quarter. [55]

[55] See Table 3.10 and M. Abramovitz and V.F. Eliasberg, *The Growth of Public Employment in Great Britain,* Princeton 1957, p. 63, Table 7.

The explanations of the Civil Service Commission for the increase in staff do not make it easy to decide whether there was bulging, or whether it was a matter of extending services which the authorities considered essential. The Commission's reports, in particular for the early years, give the impression that the civil service grew at a dizzying speed and unchecked, and that the number of unnecessary workers was large; on the other hand the failure to reduce the staff, absolutely or at least relatively, stemmed from the objective need to expand the supply of services to the public. [56]

There are several signs that if there was bulging in the period 1948–55, it was subsequently arrested. The number of government employees per 1,000 population ceased to rise after 1955 (with or without enterprises), and so did the number in general administration. This stable level was achieved despite the rise in employment in the government's social services (see Table 5.9). Moreover the proportion of civil servants in professional grades rose. [57] Both these are evidence that better use was made of a given volume of manpower, and there was thus a real expansion in the volume of services.

But the fact that the share of administrative services did not rise is not *prima facie* evidence that there was no bulging. The rise in the employment share of Jewish sector public services was explained by the need to make up the deficiency in the mandatory government's activities. [58] When the new government took over these services, the pre-State institutions actually kept their employment share—i.e., their volume rose about two and a half times in the first half of the State period. This seems to show that very serious bulging existed. Instead of contracting, these institutions acquired new functions during the period of mass immigration and were unwilling to abandon fields in which they had been active in the past. We can reasonably assume that if mass immigration had been postponed for two or three years and if employment conditions had been easier in the early years, the pre-State institutions would have been more smoothly integrated into the State system, with less redundancy and overlapping.

Because of the special character of government services (i.e. market profitability criteria do not apply) and for various other reasons discussed earlier, overconcentration may persist even after the initial conditions

[56] Civil Service Commission, *Seventh Report, 1956/57*, 1958, p. 19 (Hebrew).
[57] In 1955 there were 3,731 persons in professional grades (excluding teachers) and 18,289 administrative civil servants. In 1961 the corresponding figures were 8,815 and 20,165 (CBS, *SAI 1963*, No. 14, p. 543, Table 40.)
[58] See pp. 115–17.

for its creation have passed, and has probably done so to the present.

One further comment is required. Direct or indirect government control of various enterprises in all branches of the economy is liable to lead to the employment of too many workers in these branches as well. The most striking example is the unemployment relief works which employed thousands of workers.[59] Similar, less obvious, examples can be found. The Bank of Israel's *Annual Report 1955* speaks of manufacturing as affected by disguised unemployment.

Conditions for the emergence of bulging existed during the mandatory period and in the first half of the State period. In the mandatory period trade and personal services were the principal points of bulging. After the establishment of the State, the emphasis shifted to general government. In recent years most of the conditions for the creation of bulging have disappeared; in particular the rate of population and labour force growth has declined, and there is full employment. The data show a corresponding decline in bulging in trade and personal services, and the number of government employees has ceased its relative growth. It is, however, difficult to say how far bulging has disappeared from government services.

6. SUMMARY

The main findings of this chapter are summarized in Chapter 6. We here confine ourselves to saying that the analysis for 1961 is, in general, borne out and confirmed by the developments of 1931–61.

The period findings seem to support the import surplus explanation, changes in the degree and structure of services overconcentration parallelling changes in the volume and structure of the import surplus.

The correspondence between the growth of the public sector (in particular general government) and the growth in its resources is especially interesting. This was accompanied by changes in objective needs (for example, the effect of demographic changes on education and health requirements), and in the ruling ideology.

The availability of professional manpower (especially of doctors) has left its mark throughout the period, and changes in supply have affected the level of the services supplied.

Some of the factors found during the period were inactive in 1961. This explains some of the differences in composition between 1961 and the rest of the period.

[59] D. Patinkin, *op. cit.*, p. 32, Table 7.

Chapter 6: Conclusion

1. SUMMARY AND EVALUATION

The share of services in Israel is markedly higher than in other countries with a similar level of per capita national income. This is reflected by both the employment and the product share, (although for the latter, income level was not found to be a very meaningful criterion). However, the product-worker ratio of Israel is similar to that of other countries in the same income group.

There is overconcentration mainly in public administration, education, health, and other public services, in transportation, and possibly, finance. There is no overconcentration in trade and personal services.

An international comparison based on total resources rather than national income explains a small but significant part of the services overconcentration found in Israel. Small—because an increase of $ 190 (the difference between per capita product and resources) in per capita income can lead to only a relatively small rise in the employment share of services, and because an increase in per capita national income will have an effect different from that of an increase in per capita income from foreign sources.

The substitution effect of the import surplus, which stems the fact that the import surplus is goods-intensive, can explain most of the overconcentration in Israel's services. When the import surplus is added to GNP, the industrial structure of the economy is found to be much like that of other countries at the same stage of development.

The income effect and the substitution effect of the import surplus together are reflected mainly in the overconcentration in administration and other public services in Israel. The income effect—because the bulk of the capital import which finances the import surplus flows to the public sector; and the substitution effect—because the import surplus includes a considerable element of trade, transportation and other commercial services, but few other services.

Public and business services are mostly supplied by government and nonprofit institutions: it is relatively easy for them to supplement tax revenue, especially from foreign sources; there is, too, the government's interventionist and welfare-state approach, partly imposed by objective needs; these made possible, and indeed induced, the creation of an 'optimum public budget' much higher than is usual in other countries, and are the direct cause of overconcentration of employment and product in the public sector.

It was found that the education burden imposed on the adult population of Israel is one of the highest, if not the highest, in the world. This is due principally to the combination of a 'young' demographic structure with high educational standards.

Somewhat similar conclusions were reached in regard to health services. In addition, we have here relatively low efficiency, due mainly to the oversupply of doctors and the shortage of hospital facilities.

We have explored many of the factors which produce the overconcentration in general government services employment, but it is difficult to determine the contribution of each. The overconcentration may be explained by the necessity to administer the considerable funds at the disposal of the public sector. Other possibly explanatory factors are: invisible exports of government services to Jews in the Diaspora; the economies of scale to be reaped by government activities in spheres which a small economy cannot exploit; the organizational shortcomings of the institutional structure of government, and the overlapping of functions implict in the institutional history of the mandatory period; and an element of disguised unemployment may have carried over from the days of mass immigration and unemployment in the early 1950's.

Since there is an obvious connexion between import surplus and the other factors causing employment overconcentration in education, health, and administration, the various effects are not additive. Nonetheless, the factors at work in education, health, and administration would find some expression even if there were no import surplus.

Overconcentration in services was more marked at the beginning and in the course of the period than at its end. During the Mandate, overconcentration of employment was accompanied by a lower product-worker ratio than was to be expected from the comparison with other countries. Throughout the period we find a very moderate rise, absolutely and compared with other countries, in the employment share of services; at the same time, there was a relatively moderate decline in product per worker. This happened despite the dynamic economic development of the period, in particular the high rate of growth of per capita income, and the even higher rate of growth of the labour force.

In contrast to the situation in 1961, at the beginning and during the period overconcentration of employment was in trade and personal services and not (during the mandatory period) in government services. Throughout the whole period there was also overconcentration in other public services, and it appeared in general government in the first years after the establishment of the State. The low product-worker ratio in public services during the Mandate, and in trade after the second world war and until the mid-1950's, is especially noteworthy.

The principal divergences from other countries in the development of services are the sharp declines in the employment shares of trade and personal services which occurred at the end of the period. As in other countries, we see in Israel a rise in the employment share of public services (especially general government), as well as in finance and transport.

The corresponding changes in product per worker are a decline in trade throughout most of the period (as in other countries) with a rise at the end (unlike in other countries); there was also a decline in finance (with a rise at the end of the period) and in transportation. In personal services, general government and other public services the ratio rose. In the latter the change is in the opposite direction to what is found elsewhere, but considering the low starting level, this only means that the situation has become more similar to what it is abroad.

Broadly speaking, the development of services in Israel over the last thirty years may be explained mainly by two factors: first, the rise in the employment share of services and the decline in the product-worker ratio which result from the increase in per capita national income; and second, a combination of factors peculiar to Israel which led to overconcentration in services and to the relatively low product-worker ratio in these branches; the combined influence of these factors was stronger at the beginning than at the end of the period. These two opposing tendencies produced the moderate rise in the share of persons employed in services, and the moderate decline in the product-worker ratio.

The considerable import surplus, which explains most of the 1961 overconcentration, persisted, and therefore provides an explanation, throughout the period. The further back one goes in time, the greater the weight of the import surplus. Other features of foreign trade at the beginning of the period were: the high share of foreign trade in resources, 'foreign' trade with the Arab sector, and the Middle East transit trade. These further explain the overconcentration in services—and with greater cogency, the further back one goes.

Since 1948, the combined effect of resources available to the public sector, the functions it undertook, and the objective demand for certain public services (education, health, welfare) has become more important. The transfer of regime was a crucial factor in this change. The limited (and perhaps restricting) functions of the Mandatary and the difficulties of the Jewish sector institutions in mobilizing resources were among the more important brakes on public sector employment and economic activity during the Mandate. These influences were to some extent mitigated by considerable private demand and partial private financing.

Two factors of importance in raising services employment in the first part of the period up to the middle 1950's, but whose effect was weakened or almost non-existent by 1961, were :

a. Bulging—or overconcentration in services resulting from the difficulties of 'productive' branches in absorbing additional manpower. The conditions for this phenomenon—a rate of population growth in excess of the growth potential of 'productive' branches—prevailed until the mid-1950's, and have been disappearing since.

b. The occupational structure of the immigrants. A high proportion of immigrants were in the liberal professions (especially during the Mandate) and commercial occupations (throughout the period). This also conduced to overconcentration in services—whether because of the difficulties of entering other occupations, or (especially in the liberal professions) because of lack of occupational mobility.

The relatively strong bulging effect and the oversupply of professional manpower were combined with the effect of the import surplus in the first part of the period, while in 1961 the import surplus was decisive. This explains why the product-worker ratio was low in comparison to other countries at the beginning of the period, but not at its end.

Bulging, the occupational structure of immigration, and some of the features of the Jewish sector's external relations explain the severe overconcentration in trade in the first part of the period. Bulging explains mainly the overconcentration in personal services. The relatively low product-worker ratio in trade since the end of the second world war, with its rise in the last few years, and the fact that the ratio for personal services was higher in the State than in the mandatory period, confirm these explanations. It is harder to account in this way for the relatively high product-worker ratio of trade before the second world war.

The points mentioned earlier, taken together with the various conditions for the creation of bulging in general government when the State was established—and for the continued existence of the institutions of the emergent State—explain both the small share of general government during the Mandate, and its high share in the State.

The oversupply of professional manpower must also be taken into account in order to understand the overconcentration in public services of the mandatory period. During the period of the State, the considerable public demand for these services, due both to increased needs and increased resources, were of greater importance. This is confirmed by the rise in the product-worker ratio of these services from the mandatory to the State period.

The factors explaining overconcentration in services during the period surveyed fall into three categories:

a. Explanations which assume that Israel's demand structure—in the sense of allocation of demand to goods or services—is normal. Under this head we have mainly the income and substitution effects of the import surplus, and other foreign trade effects.

b. Explanations which assume that Israel's demand structure is not normal, but tends to prefer services to goods, principally owing to the demand of the public sector and its weight in the economy. This category includes the factors which explain the large public sector share in the economy.

c. Explanations in terms of various factors stemming from the pressure of manpower supply, and the low level of productivity in several service branches. This category includes bulging, the occupational structure of immigration, and the institutional structure of the public sector.

Factors of type a. (neutral) and type c. (supply) were the main influences operating during the mandatory period. Type b. (demand) became operative in the early days of the State, while supply factors declined in importance from the mid-1950's on. In 1961 most of the overconcentration is explained by neutral and demand factors, while supply factors have, it seems, only a small effect. In this sense, we believe that, despite the services-intensive branch structure of the economy, it is possible to speak of the success of Zionist ideology. We will not attempt to determine how far this success is due to deliberate efforts made by its proponents or to independent economic forces.

We shall not enter into any profound discussion of Israel's economy from the optimum structure point of view. Clearly, in so far as bulging or relative inefficiency still exist, they are not positive features. Economists representing different economic systems do not agree about the optimum share of general government services, even when it results from demand pressures. There is today virtually no difference of opinion on the immense economic importance of a high educational and health level or of the supply of other social services, and they have priority over a long list of commodities produced by 'productive' branches. Lastly, the adaptation of the economy's industrial structure to the existence of the import surplus is after all only behaviour that accords with undoubted economic criteria.

2. FORECAST

In order to outline the developments of the next decade we assume:

a. The present rapid growth of GNP and GNP per capita will continue (9 to 11 per cent and 4 to 6 per cent a year respectively, in recent years).

b. The ratio of import surplus to total resources will decline; this is because the import surplus will grow more slowly—if at all—than product. At the same time, the resources on which the public sector is able to draw in excess of tax revenue will decline relatively, and perhaps even absolutely.

c. Immigration will continue at a rate no higher than in recent years, so that the labour force will grow annually by no more than 4 to 5 per cent, and we assume that this is consistent with full employment.

Our findings and these assumptions might enable us to say:

a. The rapid growth of per capita national income will lead to an increase in the employment share of trade and finance. This emerges from the international studies, as well as from the fact that in recent years trade has reached a normal level, and can continue to develop along the usual lines. The recent years' (abnormal) rise in the product-worker ratio confirms this conjecture. As we have seen, the import surplus hardly affects the volume of trade and finance.

b. For the same reason (rapid growth of per capita income), the volume of personal services is expected to rise. It appears that the employment share of domestic services has already reached a very low level, and that other personal services and recreation will in future have greater weight, and that there will be a rise in their employment share. The development of tourism is also likely to contribute to this trend, while the relative decline in the import surplus will hold back expansion.

c. Various factors acting in opposing directions will affect the volume of public services: the decline in the weight of the import surplus and the relative decline in the non-tax resources available to the public sector will slow down its growth; on the other hand, the rise in per capita income (and with it, in the tax potential) will offset this tendency. Other retarding factors are: (i) Full employment, which can assist the government and the institutions in reducing general government's share of manpower. (ii) Some reduction in requirements of certain services such as welfare and, perhaps, health. (iii) Only in the longer run will it be possible to return to a normal level of health services—when these are firmly based on an advanced hospital system, and perhaps also after a relative decline in the supply of doctors.

On the other hand, no reduction in the education burden of the economy is to be expected in the near future. Although the proportion of school-age population will drop slightly, a further intensification of the educational system is to be expected. On the whole, it seems that there will be a rather small decline in the share of public services and a greater one in the share of general government.

One reservation must be made. In this forecast we assume that the import surplus declines (relatively) because foreign resource mobilization opportunities are reduced, and because of the country's progress towards economic independence. In so far as the exogenous restraint on additional resources is elastic, the government has plenty of leeway in deciding on how far to allocate the resources to public services. Moreover, to the extent that services overconcentration indicates inefficiency, and hence a slowing down of economic advance, it may itself impede the reduction of the import surplus. As this study has shown, inefficiency is only partly reflected in the present structure of services.

d. It is difficult to forecast changes in transportation and public utilities. It seems that a combination of all forces will result in there being no marked changes in the share of transportation.

e. For all services together we expect a rise in the employment shares of trade, finance and personal services, and a decline in the share of public services. We believe that these changes will more or less offset each other, so that the aggregate importance of services in the economy will remain stable. In the other branches, we expect industry to increase its share at the expense of agriculture, and to some degree also of construction. The higher per capita national income which will prevail in, say, 1970 will in itself explain a large part of the volume of services, and there will thus be a smaller degree of overconcentration.[1]

---

[1] A crude idea of the 1970 picture may be as follows: per capita national income of $ 950–$ 1,000 resulting from a 5 per cent per annum growth, will explain 44 to 45 per cent of the 50 per cent envisaged as the share of services. An import surplus of $ 100 per capita can explain about one half of the overconcentration, the other half being attributable to strong public sector demand for public services.

Appendix A:

ECONOMIC CLASSIFICATION

The data were classified as far as possible in accordance with the standard economic classification (SEC) of the CBS,[1] summarized below. In order to save space in the text tables, each item has been given a shortened description, here italicized, which applies to the whole of the group indicated.

SEC code		Description
Order [2]	*Major branch* [2]	
0		*Agriculture* forestry and fishing
1		Mining and quarrying ⎱ *Industry*
2–3		Manufacturing ⎰
4		*Construction* and public works
5		*Public utilities:* Electricity, water and sanitary services
7		*Transportation,* storage and communication
	70	*Railways*
	71	*Road passenger transport* ⎱ *Road* ⎱ *Inland transport-*
	72	*Road haulage* ⎰ *transportation* ⎰ *ation*
	73, 74	*Shipping* and port services
	75	*Aviation:* Air transport including airport services
	78	*PTT:* Communications (posts, telephone, telegraph)
	76, 77	*Other transportation* including storage
6		*Commerce*
	60	*Wholesale trade* ⎱ *trade*
	61–66	*Retail trade* (including pedlars) ⎰
	67	*Banking* and finance ⎱ *finance*
	68, 69	*Insurance* and real estate ⎰
8		*Public* and business *services*
	80–83	*General government*
	80	*Central government*
	81	*Local authorities*

[1] Classification of Economic Branches, Census of Population and Housing 1961 Publication No. 2, 1961, (Hebrew).

[2] We do not use this terminology, but refer loosely to 'branches' and sub-branches.

Appendix A (cont.)

SEC code		Description
Order	*Major branch*	
	82	*National institutions* ⎫ *National*
	83	*Trade* and other *organizations* [3] ⎬ *institutions, etc.*
	84–89	*Other public* and business *services*
	84	*Educational* services
	85	*Health* services
	86	*Welfare* services
	87	*Religious institutions*
	88	*Business* and legal *services*
	89	*Other community services*
9		*Personal services* and recreation
	90	*Recreation* and sport services
	91	*Domestic services*
	92	*Restaurants* and other drinking and ⎫ *Catering*
		eating services ⎬ *services*
	93	*Hotels* and other lodging places ⎭
	94	*Laundries* and cleaning services
	95	*Barbers* and beauty parlours
	99	*Other personal services*
	—	Personal and municipal services in *kibbutzim*

[3] Labour associations; trade, economic, and professional associations; and political parties.

Appendix B:

The 1952–61 product figures are from CBS, *Israel's National Income
and Expenditure (1950–1962)*, Special Series No. 153, Jerusalem, 1964,
referred to as NAD. In order to reconcile the product and employment
figures, the source items were fitted into the LFS classification scheme
(see Appendix A) as follows:

Table number and description in NAD		LFS item
58	Agriculture, forestry and fishing	0
58	Manufacturing, mining and quarrying	1, 2–3
58	Construction	4
58	Public utilities	5
58	Transportation and communication	7
69	Road passenger transport	71
69	Road haulage	72
69	Shipping and port services	73
69	Ports	74
69	Air transport and airports	75
69	Railways	70
69	Posts	78
58	Trade	
72	Wholesale trade	60
72	Retail trade	61–66
58	Finance, insurance and real estate	
70	Commercial banks and cooperative credit societies	67
70	Insurance, provident funds, and other financial institutions	68, 69
71	General government	
71	Private nonprofit institutions and miscellaneous	8 [a]
58	Other services	
73	Health	85
73	Legal and auditing	88
73	Engineering and architecture	88
73	Recreation and entertainment	90
73	Hotels, restaurants and cafes	92, 93
73	Personal services	84, 91, 94, 99 [b]
73	Other services	Kibbutzim, 88, 2–3 [b]

[a] This item was broken down in detail according to various sources.
[b] According to unpublished NAD detail.

Appendix C:

THE EDUCATION-BURDEN IN SELECTED COUNTRIES[a]

	Per cent of population aged 5–19	Per cent of 5–19 age-group attending school[b]	Pupils per teacher in primary schools	Per cent of population	
				Attending school[b] (1) × (2)	Teachers (4) ÷ (3)
	(1)	(2)	(3)	(4)	(5)
Uganda	33	23	29	7.6	0.26
Burma	33	27	42[c]	8.9	0.21
India	34	28	34	9.5	0.28
Belgian Congo	29	30	40	8.7	0.22
Pakistan	35	19	37	6.7	0.18
South Korea	36	50	58	18.0	0.31
Thailand	37	44	34	16.3	0.48
Egypt	35	34	38	11.9	0.31
Peru	37	39	36	14.4	0.40
Paraguay	33	50	29	16.5	0.57
Honduras	39	25	32	9.8	0.31
Ecuador	36	39	39	14.0	0.36
Philippines	39	48	37[c]	18.7	0.51
Guatemala	36	21	29	7.6	0.26
Dominican Republic	38	51	80	19.4	0.24
Jamaica	32	52	52	16.6	0.32
Japan	33	77	35	25.4	0.73
Portugal	27	43	35[c]	11.6	0.33
Mexico	44	40	45	17.6	0.39
Greece	25	54[d]	44	13.5	0.31
Brazil	36	38	35	13.7	0.40
Panama	37	51	30	18.9	0.63
Colombia	33	34	39	11.2	0.29
South Africa	30	51	30	15.3	0.51
Cuba	33	41	35	13.5	0.39
Italy	24	51	24	12.2	0.51
Chile	34	57	47[c]	19.4	0.41
Austria	22	60	22	13.2	0.60
Ireland	28	76	35[c]	21.3	0.61
Puerto Rico	38	74	59	28.1	0.48
Argentina	28	56	23	15.7	0.68

THE EDUCATION-BURDEN IN SELECTED COUNTRIES[a] (Cont.)

	Per cent of population aged 5–19	Per cent of 5–19 age-group attending school[b]	Pupils per teacher in primary schools	Per cent of population	
				Attending school[b] (1) × (2)	Teachers (4) ÷ (3)
	(1)	(2)	(3)	(4)	(5)
Netherlands	28	69	34	19.3	0.57
West Germany	21	81	33	17.0	0.52
Venezuela	36	51	36	18.4	0.51
Finland	28	69	23	19.3	0.84
France	20	76	29	15.2	0.52
Denmark	26	73	33	19.0	0.58
United Kingdom	22	78	29	17.2	0.59
Belgium	21	72	24	15.1	0.63
Luxembourg	18	50	26[c]	9.0	0.35
Sweden	23	71	19	16.3	0.86
Australia	27	77	31	20.8	0.67
New Zealand	27	77	32	20.8	0.65
Switzerland	22	61	26[c]	13.4	0.52
Canada	27	80	30	21.6	0.72
United States	27	83	31	22.4	0.72
Israel	32	69	24	22.1	0.92

[a] Countries are ranked by per capita income. Most of the data are for one of the years 1957 through 1960; data for Ecuador, Jamaica, Chile, Argentina, France and Switzerland are for one of the years 1950 through 1954.
[b] Primary and secondary schools.
[c] Public schools.
[d] Excludes vocational schools and teacher training.
SOURCE: Column (1) relevant issues of UN, *Demographic Yearbook.*
Columns (2) and (3)—UNESCO, *Basic Facts and Figures, 1956,* Tables 2 and 3; and *1961,* Tables 2 and 4.

Bibliography

Abramovitz, M., and Eliasberg V. F., *The Growth of Public Employment in Great Britain*, NBER, Princeton, 1957.

Bauer, P. T., and Yamey, B. S., "Economic Progress and Occupational Distribution," *The Economic Journal*, LXI (December 1951), 741–55.

Brown, E. H. P., *The Economics of Labor*, Yale University Press, New Haven, 1962.

Bruno, Michael, *Interdependence, Resource Use, and Structural Change in Israel*, Bank of Israel Research Department, Special Studies No. 2, Jerusalem, 1962.

CBS, *Labor Force—Part I*, Population and Housing Census 1961 Publication No. 9, Jerusalem, 1963.

Civil Service Commission, *Seventh Report 1956/57*, 1958 (Hebrew).

Clark, Colin, *The Conditions of Economic Progress* (third ed.), London, 1957.

Economic Advisory Staff, *The Israel Economy in 1954*, Jerusalem, 1955 (mimeograph).

Epstein, T. S., "European Contact and Tolai Economic Development: A Schema of Economic Growth," *Economic Development and Cultural Change*, XI (April 1963), 289–307.

Fabricant, S., *Trends in Government Activity Since 1900*, NBER, New York, 1952.

Gaathon, A. L., "National Income," *Encyclopaedia Hebraica*, VI (1957), 729–39, (Hebrew).

—, *Survey of Israel's Economy 1951*, FP and CBS Technical Paper No. 1, Jerusalem, 1959.

Gruenbaum (Gaathon), L., *National Income and Outlay in Palestine 1936*, Jerusalem, 1941.

—, *Outlines of a Development Plan for Palestine*, Jewish Agency Economic Research Institute, 1946.

Halevi, N., and Klinov-Malul, R., *The Development of the Israel Economy*, (forthcoming).

Hanoch, Giora, "Income Differentials in Israel," *Fifth Report 1959 and 1960*, FP, Jerusalem, 1961.

Horowitz, D., *The Economy of Palestine and its Development*, (revised ed.), 1948.

Hovne, Avner, *The Labor Force in Israel*, FP, Jerusalem, 1961.

Jaffe, A. G., *People, Jobs and Economic Development*, The Free Press of Glencoe, Illinois, 1959.

Jewish Agency, "The Occupational Structure of Jewish Earners," *Alon Statisti*, Vol. I, 1–6, June 1946 (Hebrew).

—, *Statistical Handbook of Jewish Palestine 1947*, Department of Statistics, Jerusalem, 1947.

Kessler, Avraham, "The Balance of Payments," *Encyclopaedia Hebraica*, VI (1957), 745–52, (Hebrew).

Kuznets, S., "Quantitative Aspects of the Economic Growth of Nations, I. Levels and Variability of Rates of Growth," *Economic Development and Cultural Change,* V (No. 1, October 1956).

—, "Quantitative Aspects of the Economic Growth of Nations, II. Industrial Distribution of National Product and Labor Force," *Economic Development and Cultural Change,* V (supplement to No. 4, July 1957).

—, "Quantitative Aspects of the Economic Growth of Nations, III. Industrial Distribution of Income and Labor Force by States, United States, 1919–1921 to 1955," *Economic Development and Cultural Change,* VI (No. 4 part II, July 1958).

—, *Six Lectures on Economic Growth,* The Free Press of Glencoe, Illinois, (1959).

—, "Economic Growth of Small Nations," in *Economic Consequences of the Size of Nations,* (ed. E. A. G. Robinson), London, 1960, pp. 14–32.

Loftus, P. J., *National Income of Palestine 1944,* Government Printer, 1946.

—, *National Income of Palestine 1945,* Government Printer, 1948.

Michaely, M., *Foreign Trade and Capital Import in Israel,* Am Oved, Tel Aviv, 1963 (Hebrew).

Nathan, R. R., Gass, Oscar, and Creamer, D., *Palestine: Problem and Promise,* Public Affairs Press, Washington, 1946.

Nizan, A., "The Structure of the Labor Force in the Israel Economy," *Economic Quarterly,* III (No. 9–10, October 1955), 58–66 (Hebrew).

Oshima, H.T., "Share of Government in Gross National Product for Various Countries," *The American Economic Review,* XLVII (June 1957), 381–90.

Patinkin, D., *The Israel Economy: The First Decade,* FP, Jerusalem, 1960.

Public Committee (I. Kanev), *Plan for General Health Insurance in Israel, 1959.*

Riemer, S., "Wages in Israel," *Encyclopaedia Hebraica,* VI (1957), 802–807.

Sicron, M., *Immigration to Israel: 1948–1953,* FP and CBS Special Series No. 60, Jerusalem, 1957.

Stigler, G. J., *Trends in Employment in the Service Industries,* NBER, Princeton, 1956.

Subject Index

National income, 7–9 *passim*, 37, 40, 45; and government activity, 37; and resources (qv), 40; classification, 8–9, 13, 79n; depreciation and stock valuation adjustment, 15, 98n; estimates, 7, 79, 119; growth or size, 4, 148; increment and external increment, 41–43, 143; industrial origin of (see also Product share), 1, 42, 44, 49; product share, qv, see also entries for various industries

National income per capita, 27, 43, 132; and educational services (qv), 61, 63; and employment share (qv), 20, 22–23, 28n, 31–32, 36, 38–40, 65, 143, 145; and foreign trade (qv), 113; and government revenue, 55–56, 59; and industrial structure (qv), 1, 16–23, 103, 148; and economic development (qv), 2, 8, 16–17, 39, 55; and product share (qv), 16, 19, 21–23, 26, 28–29, 30–31, 33, 143; and product-worker ratio (qv), 27–28, 32, 37–38, 143, 145; growth or size, 1, 4, 23, 102–103, 138, 144, 148–49; in international comparisons, 8, 16–17, 39, 60, 134, 143; see also National income

National institutions, 72, 111, 117–19, 136, 141, 148; defined, 36n; employment share, 35–36, 93, 139, 141; income of, 58; see also Government services, general, Public services

Netherlands, 26n, 44n, 113

New Zealand, 26n, 65n, 134–35

Non-Jewish sector, see Arab sector

Nonprofit institutions, 8, 53, 58–59, 143; product share, 6; provision of health services (qv) by, 66; see also Public services

Norway, 29n, 63, 113, 134–35

Occupational mobility, structure, of immigrants, see Immigrants

Occupational structure of Jewish sector,

labour force, see Jewish sector, Labour force

OS sector, see 'Other services'

'Other public services', see Public services

'Other services', 31–37 *passim*; employment share, 22, 30, 38, 41n, 57, 106; import surplus effects (qv) in, 41n, 43, 50, 53; product share, 30–33, 36–37, 43, 106; product-worker ratio, 23, 27, 32–33, 106; see also Personal services, Public services

Palestine, partition of, 4, 83

Panama, 53

Participation income, 6

Per capita national income, product, see National income per capita

Per capita resources, see Resources per capita

Personal services, 5, 21, 77, 101, 108, 112, 143, 148; and bulging (qv), 131, 133n, 137, 139, 142, 146; employment share, 9, 31, 33, 37, 43, 94–95, 101, 107, 139, 144–45, 149; product share, 8–9, 36–37, 79, 84, 95, 101; product-worker ratio, 15, 37, 98, 100–101, 139, 145; see also Catering, Domestic services, 'Other services'

Police, 36, 74, 93–94, 100, 140

Political stream system, 129n

Population, 76; age-structure of, 17, 60–61, 63–64, 127, 129, 134, 149; censuses, 2–3, 9, 13, 15, 25, 27, 30n, 35n, 85–86, 90, 93, 95, 139; density, 55n, 73; growth (see also Labour force growth), 3–4, 39, 120, 132, 134–37, 142, 146; size and foreign trade (qv), 113; see also Demographic structure

Port services, see Transportation

PTT (communications), 73–74, 115, 117, 131; employment share, 73;

Name Index